HENK VAN OORT, born in 1
teacher before taking a Maste
Amsterdam University. He has taught for 40 years in primary and secondary education, including class teaching in a Steiner school, teaching English, and running educational courses and seminars for teachers and parents. Henk van Oort's interest in literature and poetry has led to him appearing at storytelling and poetry seminars, and his introductory courses to anthroposophy have proved to be highly successful. Based in Bergen N.H. in the Netherlands, he is married and the father of three grown-up children.

Anthroposophy

A concise introduction to Rudolf Steiner's spiritual philosophy

Henk van Oort

TEMPLE LODGE

Temple Lodge Publishing
Hillside House, The Square
Forest Row, RH18 5ES

www.templelodge.com

Published in English by Temple Lodge 2008

Originally published in Dutch under the title *Antroposofie, Een kennismaking* by Vrij Geestesleven, Zeist 2006

A catalogue record for this book is available from the British Library

ISBN 978 1902636 92 4

Cover design by Andrew Morgan
Typeset by DP Photosetting, Neath, West Glamorgan
Printed and bound by Cromwell Press Limited, Trowbridge, Wiltshire

Contents

Prologue

Ovid (43 BC–AD 18) describes in his *Metamorphoses* how Aeneas travels to the Sanctuary of Apollo at Cumae, not far from Naples in Italy, to gain access to the spiritual world in order to consult the soul of his deceased father. The Sibyl, one of the priestesses of Apollo who guard the sanctuary, shows Aeneas a Golden Bough which he is told to break off the tree. This Golden Bough will allow Aeneas to enter the spiritual world and there meet up with the spirit of his dead father. The scene has been beautifully depicted by the English painter William Turner (1775–1851). This oil painting is now to be seen in the Tate Britain gallery in London.

Following Aeneas' visit many people also visited this remarkable spot in Italy. Amongst others, Hannibal, Tsar Nicholas I and Mussolini's wife: they all came to experience something of another world beyond the physical world, hoping to find an answer to the deepest questions life presents us with.

These same lines from Ovid's *Metamorphoses* inspired James Frazer to write his famous book *The Golden Bough*, published in 1890. This work comprises 12 volumes and is an extraordinarily extensive collection of mythology, magic and religious ideas from all parts of the world.

This concise introduction to Rudolf Steiner's anthroposophy—the word itself means 'wisdom of man'—would like to be a modern *Golden Bough*, a helping hand for readers in their search for the source and the aim of life on earth.

1. A Biography of Rudolf Steiner (1861–1925)

Early childhood

Rudolf Steiner was born on 27 February 1861, of Austrian parents, in the village of Kraljevec in present-day Croatia, then Hungary. His father was an employee of the national railways and worked in the village. Two days after his birth Rudolf Steiner was baptized into the Roman Catholic Church. Soon after, the family moved to Pottschach and after a short period of time they moved again, this time to the Hungarian village of Neudörfl, not far from Wiener-Neustadt.

In his childhood Steiner greatly enjoyed the mountains and the forests he was surrounded by. He also took an extraordinary interest in all technology related to trains and railway stations. After Rudolf, a son and a daughter were born into the family.

From a very early age Steiner was aware of the existence of two worlds: a visible and an invisible world. At the age of eight he had a clairvoyant experience in the waiting-room of the station in Pottschach, about which he did not dare to speak with anyone. The child did not know what to do with this experience, but it was the start of a rapidly developing inborn faculty.

When he was a pupil in primary education and could lay his hands on a geometry book, he recognized in that world also a kind of invisible realm. In Steiner's *Autobiography* we can read:

> *'Being able to grasp something in mere spiritual circumstances gave me an inner happiness. I know that I have experienced happiness for the first time through geometry.'*

And a little further on:

> *'When at work with geometry I said to myself: here you are allowed to know something that only the soul experiences through its own power; in this feeling I found a justification to speak about the spiritual world much the same as I would do about the sensory world.'* (Chapters 29–30.)

From 11 to 18

When 11 years of age, in 1872, Rudolf Steiner travelled every day to the Realschule in Wiener-Neustadt, sometimes on foot, sometimes by train. The child who was so familiar with nature found it rather difficult to get used to all the new impressions of life in a big town. Steiner, however, turned out to be an excellent pupil. He was not only interested in geometry, which may be demonstrated by his keen interest in Immanuel Kant's *Critique of Pure Reason* which he bought in a pocket edition at the age of 14. From the age of 15 he coached fellow students and when he was 18 he passed his exams with credit, before becoming a student of the Technical High School in Vienna. Meanwhile he also studied all sorts of philosophical works. Because of his double perception of reality Steiner was confronted with a real problem:

> *'To me a world full of spiritual beings was real. I took for granted that the human ego, which in itself is a spiritual entity, lives in a spiritual world. Nature, however, would not fit into this spiritual world.'* (From Steiner's *Autobiography*, Chapter 30.)

Steiner was able to follow the ego of a deceased person when on its journey through the spiritual world between two lives. For a long time it remained a problem as to how he could combine this gift with his perception of the physical world.

Vienna Technical High School

In 1879 Steiner enrolled as a student at the Technical High School in Vienna. Amongst his teachers he encountered Karl Julius Schröer (German Literature) and Robert Zimmermann (Philosophy). The word 'anthroposophy' derives from Robert Zimmermann. Karl Julius Schröer roused in Steiner an interest in Goethe. This same professor managed to save the 'Oberufer Christmas Plays' from extinction. Steiner recognized the importance of these plays and until the present day they are being performed at Waldorf schools throughout the world.

Taking his PhD

On finishing his studies Steiner started working as a private teacher and in 1889, at the age of 28, he got a job at the Goethe and Schiller Archives. He edited a new edition of Goethe's scientific writings. In 1891 he obtained his PhD from the University of Rostock. Subsequently his philosophical dissertation was published in a slightly altered version with the title *Wahrheit and Wissenschaft* (Truth and Science).

From theosophy to anthroposophy

In September 1900, Rudolf Steiner gave his first lecture in the Theosophical Library at the house of Count and Countess Brockdorff in Berlin. Those who heard him, an audience consisting of theosophists, were enthralled. Many more lectures were to follow. In 1902, in the presence of Annie Besant, Steiner was asked to become secretary of the newly established German branch of the Theosophical Movement. He accepted this task but stressed that he must have the freedom to speak about his own spiritual experiences as well. The difference, however, between Steiner's approach and the ideas that Annie Besant and Helena Petrovna Blavatsky had been propagating under the name of Theosophy since 1875 proved to be too great. When in 1913 Annie Besant in effect declared Krishnamurti the new-born Christ, the rift was a fact.

In the same year the Anthroposophical Movement was established, whereby anthroposophy became a purely western European phenomenon, which was why Steiner decided to define all anthroposophical concepts in German. The terms used until that time had been borrowed from Asian religious terminology.

Lectures

From 1906 onwards Steiner delivered a series of lectures in Germany and abroad. He travelled, amongst other places, to Berlin, Stuttgart, Leipzig, Bremen, Paris, Kassel, Basle, Stockholm, Copenhagen, Budapest, Vienna, Rome, Palermo, Prague, Bologna, Milan, Arnhem, Amsterdam and London. An impressive programme indeed. Besides the organizers that travelled with him Steiner was also accompanied by a group of faithful followers. Wherever he was to appear hotels were fully booked. Most lectures were taken down in shorthand and were published in the *Gesamtausgabe* (Complete Works), which comprises 354 volumes. Furthermore books, essays, courses and facsimiles of his drawings have been published over the years.

Books

Of all the books Rudolf Steiner wrote, three titles form a sort of basis of anthroposophy. These are: *Theosophy* (1904), *Knowledge of the Higher Worlds* (1904) and *Occult Science* (1910).

Theosophy

In this book the visible and invisible parts of man are discussed. At the same time the reader gains some insight into the world which follows death and lasts until the next incarnation. The concepts of *karma* and *reincarnation* are extensively dealt with.

Knowledge of the Higher Worlds

This book presents the reader with a vast number of practical exercises with which he can further develop the higher powers that will enable him to witness the spiritual world. This spiritual world is shown to be the creating force behind all things visible.

In one of Steiner's exercises the student who wishes to develop his higher powers is advised to occupy himself only with the positive characteristics of those who surround him. Something similar was advised by the English diplomat and writer of *The Canterbury Tales*, Geoffrey Chaucer (1343–1400):

'Seeke out ye goode in everie man
And speke of alle the beste ye can'.

Occult Science
The long and complicated development of planet Earth is described, from the very first planetary stage until possible stages in the future. Parallel to this description we read about the development of mankind.

The last years

The centre of anthroposophical activities moved to Dornach, Switzerland, near Basle. With the help of many volunteers and artists of all nationalities Rudolf Steiner built the Goetheanum, a splendid building with two immense cupolas. Everything but the foundations was built of wood. When the foundation stone of this amazing building was laid during an impressive ceremony on 20 September 1913, Rudolf Steiner addressed the nine hierarchies of angels, and then the copper foundation stone containing a written document was entrusted to the earth.

The building was of service a few years only. It was destroyed by arson on 31 December 1922. Feelings of distress dominated the first days after the disaster. Nevertheless new initiatives saw the light of day. Rudolf Steiner made new drafts for a second Goetheanum, this time to be built of concrete. Plans were made for a large-scale meeting in Dornach during the Christmas period of 1923. At this so-called *Weinachtstagung* (Christmas Meeting) several hundred people came together in the neighbourhood of the burnt down Goetheanum. This time Rudolf Steiner laid a spiritual foundation stone, in the form of a long meditation, in the hearts and minds of the people present. This mantric text is called 'The Foundation Stone Meditation'. However, Rudolf Steiner never recovered from this fierce blow. He died on 30 March 1925. His ashes were kept until recently in the so-called *Schreinerei* (Workshop) but they have now been scattered on a special plot of land close to the Goetheanum.

Rudolf Steiner draws our attention to *The Fairy Tale of the Green Snake and the Beautiful Lily*, written by Johann Wolfgang von Goethe. In this story 'the man with the lamp' says: 'Time has come'. Steiner explains that this story is an early announcement of his anthroposophy that was yet to come. Goethe anticipated what was to happen. He felt that the time had arrived when a renewed introduction to the spiritual dimensions of the physical world would be possible.

In two lectures given on 22 and 24 October 1908, Rudolf Steiner told how Goethe, in this fairy tale, described what was happening in the spiritual world just before the French Revolution. In the tale we read about two will-o'-the-wisps, the main characters, who are searching for the White Lily. They get themselves ferried across a river but to their astonishment they hear on arrival that they have made a mistake. They have to be on the other bank, the bank they have just left. This image indicates our own situation in this earthly life. When we start searching for the 'Spiritual' we discover that we are searching on the wrong bank. We must cross the river again to find the spiritual world from which we have just come.

At the end of his life Steiner gave short definitions of anthroposophical concepts in the so-called *Leitsätze* (Leading Thoughts). Leading Thought Number One goes as follows:

> *'Anthroposophy is a path of knowledge to guide the Spiritual in the human being to the Spiritual in the universe.'*

Fields of Action

Many initiatives derive from anthroposophy. Some well-known fields of action are the following:

The second Goetheanum, Dornach.

Biodynamic agriculture and horticulture

In this kind of agriculture and horticulture inorganic material is used as little as possible. All preparations are derived from organic sources, whereby the vitality of the final product that serves as our food is enhanced. Cosmic powers are taken into consideration and actually harnessed when the preparations are made and when seeds are sown. Both man and earth benefit from this approach. Steiner introduced these concepts in his Agricultural Course, run in June 1924 in Koberwitz.

Special education

Throughout the world we find the special care centres where Steiner's ideas are put into practice. Steiner supplied the important concept that the inborn spirit of man, the ego, cannot be damaged in any way. It is the physical body that can become damaged, for whatever reason, with the result that the inborn ego cannot manifest itself to the full. If the violin is damaged even an excellent musician cannot perform Mozart as he should be played.

Medical science

Steiner has given many suggestions to enrich regular medical science. The Dutch medical doctor Ita Wegman transformed Steiner's ideas into practical initiatives. Producers of medicines such as Wala, Weleda and Dr Hauschka all work along the lines that Rudolf Steiner and Ita Wegman initiated. Steiner never practised as a doctor and he emphasized that only qualified doctors should carry out curative tasks. Anthroposophical medical science is often seen as a supplement to regular curative treatments.

Drama and speech

At the start the Goetheanum was called the 'House of Speech'. Attention was drawn to language, which was highlighted with renewed inspiration. Steiner wrote four Mystery Dramas in which he revealed to the audience all his anthroposophical ideas in an artistic form on the stage. Speech as a form of art acquired a curative aspect through the new profession of speech therapist. At all the Waldorf schools speech plays an important role in the lessons, for example in the form of choral recitation.

Eurythmy

Literally this word means 'the good rhythm'. Rudolf Steiner spoke of eurythmy as visible speech or visible singing. By means of gesture the whole body is turned into a larynx and thus every sound is represented, whether produced by a human voice or produced by a musical instrument. In this way musical compositions and human speech can be brought to expression on the stage. At the Waldorf schools the eurythmy lessons are given to all age groups.

Architecture

'Forms that awaken one to see one's own karma': thus Steiner enigmatically typifies the remarkable forms that are used in so-called 'organic architecture'. Many a time the 90-degree angle is largely avoided and whenever possible only natural materials are used. The Goetheanum in Dornach embodies these organic forms. Over the years many buildings have been built in this way throughout the world.

Education

When Emil Molt, the managing director of the Waldorf-Astoria cigarette factory in Stuttgart, Germany, asked Rudolf Steiner in 1919 how a new school system could be set up for the children of his factory staff, the first Waldorf school was established.

The curriculum comprises 12 classes and preferably all the pupils stay together during this period in the same class. All teaching material is looked upon not only as information but also as a means to further personal development. Over the years and worldwide, hundreds of Waldorf schools have been established. Meanwhile also, playgroups for the three- and four-year-olds have been set up, where the same anthroposophical way of thinking is the main source of inspiration.

The Christian Community

Finally, the Christian Community should be mentioned here. The Christian Community is part of an international movement for the renewal of religion, founded in 1922 in Switzerland by the Lutheran theologian and minister Friedrich Rittelmeyer, with the help of Rudolf Steiner. The Christian Community is a Church centred on seven sacraments in a renewed form. There are some 350 Christian Community congregations worldwide and, although not a field of action of anthroposophy such as those mentioned above, this Church finds in anthroposophy its inspiration.

2. The Fourfold Image of Man

In chapters 2, 3 and 4 we shall consider the anthroposophical concept of mankind. As mankind is such a complicated and varied phenomenon, Steiner used various approaches to explain his views. Each approach is a sort of journey through exactly the same landscape, but seen from a different and often higher hilltop each time. The higher the mountain, the more we can understand of the totality, of the mutual relationship.

Steiner tells us, for example, about the threefold and fourfold images of man. Of course, both descriptions deal with the same human being.

After having read the detailed descriptions in the following chapters, the reader will be in a position to put together the different approaches and thus create one overall concept of what, in Steiner's view, mankind is. This putting together is not always easy, but if we study and meditate on this picture of the world and its inhabitants we may unexpectedly understand a new part of the enigma. We will then have the feeling that we have climbed somewhat higher on this imaginary mountain and that we are overlooking a larger part of this impressive landscape.

* * *

Awareness of the four members of the human being may narrow down and refine our concept of mankind. The fourfold image of man plays an important role in all anthroposophical fields of action. This knowledge is essential if one wants to function in an anthroposophical way. It may be of great help not only in professional life: parents, too, will approach their children in a different way when they know something about this fourfold image of man. The *physical body,* the *ether body,* the *astral body* and the *ego* will be discussed successively.

Mineral

When we look at a stone we can make the following observations. A stone is completely subject to gravity. A stone will always be as close to the earth as possible. A stone is just itself: nothing more, nothing less. If we chip a piece off from the stone we simply have two stones. The chipped-off piece will not spontaneously change its properties. The stone, in this line of thinking, serves as a symbol for all things *mineral.* The concept of *death* can be applied here. The stone only has a *physical body.*

Plant

When we look at a plant we notice that it has an additional force that is constantly working upwards against gravity, a force striving towards the sunlight. The plant consists of mineral substance, it is true, but this elevating force, *levity*, isolates the mineral substance from gravity. When we break off a piece from a plant, a leaf or a flower, it will soon wither, disintegrate and die. The piece that was broken off cannot sustain life by itself—a huge difference compared to the stone. A ripe apple will fall from the tree with the help of gravity. But it has arrived there, high up on the tree, with the help of levity. A plant needs liquid to allow the element of life to do its work. We do not water plants just for the sake of all the minerals that find their way through the roots into the plant. We also water them to transport the element of life into the plant. This element of life is called the *ether body*. It is invisible to the untrained eye. A plant has a *physical body* and an *ether body*.

Animal

When we take a closer look at an animal, the element of movement is the most characteristic. These movements are related to all sorts of desires. Hunger, thirst, sexual drives—they are all sources of movement. An animal has a nervous system, which is the base of consciousness. An animal has feelings of discomfort and pleasure. An animal has a system that takes care of all its movements. This system is also invisible to the untrained eye. We might compare this system with the strings of a puppet. When we look at an animal in this way we notice that it has got three systems: a *physical body*, in common with a stone, an *ether body*—it is alive—in common with a plant, and a third system, which takes care of movement. This third system is called the *astral body*.

Man

When looking at a human being, we see that there is a *physical body* (in common with all things mineral), an *ether body* (in common with the world of plants) and an *astral body* (in common with animals). But in human beings there is also a fourth element: self-awareness. In anthroposophy this fourth element is called the 'I' or ego.

			ego
		astral	*astral*
	ether	*ether*	*ether*
physical	*physical*	*physical*	*physical*
stone	*plant*	*animal*	*human being*

Let us further examine this fourfold image of man.

The physical body

The mineral element is most clearly to be seen in the human skeleton and in the teeth. Although the skeleton and the teeth have come from living sources, the real element of life has gradually died away in order to create these essential parts of the human body. If too much life remained in the bones they would remain too malleable: rachitis would be the result. After death, bones and teeth are conserved longest because they are already so close to the mineral world. The physical body demonstrates its weight on the scales. It is completely subject to gravity. The human body cannot sustain life by itself. In death, the body will soon disintegrate, the shape will get lost.

There is a relationship between the physical body and what the Greek philosophers of old called the element of EARTH, *referring to all things solid.*

The ether body

The life-giving forces can only penetrate the physical body if there is an ether body that carries out this task. The ether body can only perform this when there is a liquid means of transport. The more liquid, the more ether—the more life, we could say. That is why small wounds in the mouth are cured so rapidly; there is much life due to all the saliva in the mouth. The ether body takes care of all processes related to growth. According to anthroposophy it is also the seat of habits and of memory. Ether in itself is shapeless. Just as an aquarium would empty if there was a crack in the glass, the ether body can only exist within the shape of something else—in this case, the shape of a human being.

There is a relationship between the ether body and what the Greek philosophers called the element of WATER, *referring to all things liquid.*

The astral body

Human beings, just like animals, can move due to the astral body. Also, in humans, feelings of discomfort and pleasure, of hunger and thirst, of sexual desire, are located in the astral body. Human beings, however, are able to restrain or modify these forceful powers to a greater or lesser degree. This ability is a truly human phenomenon.

The astral body of animals becomes visible in all the colours they sport—in their feathers, skin, scale, fur, etc. Steiner explains that there is a relationship between colour and the astral body. Human beings are able to suppress their own astral powers with the ego so that only very few colours come to the surface: hair, eyes, skin. The human ego modifies, reins in, the powerful influence of all things astral. If, in certain circumstances, the astral powers become too strong, human beings start to paint themselves. In the past the Picts, in the northern regions of the British Isles, were called Picts because they used to paint themselves when they waged wars, just as the Native Americans—redskins—did in North America. Application of modern tattoos has the same rationale; the astral body leaves a fierce imprint on the skin. The mood in which we get up in the morning, i.e. the feelings in our astral body at that moment of the day, decides what we are going to wear on that particular day. Children, and adults who are sensitive to such things, will notice the connection between the mood and the clothing the teacher wears in class.

The astral powers are likely to increase in places where many people live together, such as in big cities, often ending up in grotesque manifestations. In the country the astral powers are more restricted and connected to the countryside and all its ethereal vegetation and animal life. The accumulated astral powers in a big city may be felt by sensitive human beings.

There is a relationship between the astral body and what the Greek philosophers called the element of AIR, *referring to all things gaseous.*

An interesting experiment:

Stand at right angles to a wall, your right shoulder at a distance of 30 cm from the wall. Press the back of your right hand quite forcefully against the wall. The arm must be kept stretched. After 60 seconds jump to the left. You will notice that your arm goes upward all by itself, as if a puppeteer were pulling a piece of string that is attached to your arm and hand. No doubt there are many explanations for this phenomenon. In the context of this book we may say that, in the first stage, the astral body of the arm was pressed upwards. The physical arm, however, could not follow because of the wall. As soon as this obstacle disappears—when you jump away from the wall—the physical arm follows, filling in, as it were, the astral arm that is still hanging in the air.

'In towns life is of low quality.
There are too many rutting creatures.'
Friedrich Nietzsche (1844–1900), from *Also sprach Zarathustra* (Thus spoke Zarathustra)

The ego

There are several words with which we can define this fourth element. Aristotle (384–322 BC) calls it *entelechy,* the word from which 'intelligent' derives. The meaning of this Greek word is: *having the aim in itself.* A chestnut, for example, is also an entelechy: only a chestnut will grow out of it, not an oak. Likewise, from the ego, only one human being with all its characteristics can grow. Another term for this fourth element could be *persona.* The persona was the mask through which the voice of the actors in ancient Greece sounded on the stage. The meaning of the word is: *sounding through.* In this context, a person is a creature through which the entelechy can speak and make itself known. Yet another term for this fourth element is *individual.* The word means: *indivisible.* The ego is indivisible and inalienable.

In the later years of the life of a human being the ego becomes more and more visible. In elderly people we can more or less see from their outward appearance what the ego has been focusing on during the preceding stages of life.

A strong manifestation of the ego can be seen when someone blushes. The ego, present in the blood, steps out of the physical body into the element of warmth.

When two people meet they try to look at one another straight in the eye. This is a complicated matter. We rapidly and in turn look into the left and into the right eye of the other person. This activity might be indicated with a verb: 'to ego'. We try to assess what sort of person the other human being really is.

There is a relationship between the ego and what the Greek philosophers called the element of FIRE. And here FIRE refers to not only a state of aggregation but to an even more rarefied state of the element of AIR. This concept has disappeared from our present-day scientific consciousness.

The birth of the four members of a human being

The birth of the physical body

Life on earth starts with the birth of the physical body. The newborn human being must get used to earthly circumstances. In contrast to being immersed in the amniotic fluids of the womb, gravity starts taking effect upon the body and air rushes into the lungs: breathing begins. The senses must become accustomed to a welter of new impressions. From this moment all available life forces from the ether body are busy building up the physical body. This building-up process is complete when the second teeth appear, after approximately seven years.

The birth of the ether body

When this building-up process has finished, the life-giving forces of the ether body are partly freed from their task. From this moment on, the ether body maintains, rather than creates, the physical body. The surplus of ether forces becomes independent. This change is called *the birth of the ether body*. These freed life-giving forces, or ether forces, are from this moment available for the development of thinking.

The birth of the astral body

At about the age of 14 a third essential change takes place. The astral body is born; the child becomes sexually mature. Rudolf Steiner calls this stage 'earth ripe'. All astral forces get a firm grip on the individuality, which often results in a temporary state of confusion. The astral forces may be compared very well to a zoo without bars. The human ego finds itself confronted with a new task: mastering these overwhelming new forces. The birth of the astral body is an impressive event, both for the individuality and for the educators.

The growth to independence of the astral body starts about the age of seven. At that age the child is touched by the astral forces for the first time. In the curriculum of the Waldorf schools—in the second class—we find that fables and stories of saints are told to children of that age to accompany this process. Fables are chosen because these stories express the one-sidedness of animals. An animal is its own completely materialized astral body. An animal cannot do anything else than just be itself. 'An eagle catches no flies' is a well-known saying. To counterbalance this one-sidedness, the stories of saints are told because saints have learnt to master these one-sided astral forces.

St Francis is often depicted with animals, which consider him a friend, not an enemy. An individuality is called a saint because he has learnt to master all the forces that live in his own astral body.

The birth of the ego

Approximately around the age of 20, the fourth birth takes place: the ego is born, also called the *entelechy*, or *person,* or *individuality*. The inherited physical body has been reworked,

The four elements in Greek philosophy. These elements aim at being in their own appropriate places: earth below, then water covering earth, next air hovering above water, and on top fire. The elements can be recognized in the four members of a human being:

FIRE—EGO
AIR—ASTRAL BODY
WATER—ETHER BODY
EARTH—PHYSICAL BODY

has been appropriated by the ego to the best of its ability. The physical body has been reshaped into the best-fitting form for the ego to inhabit during the rest of its life. The real personality steps into the open and starts carrying out the tasks of life.

In this way four births take place. Each of them must take place at the right moment. However, due to cultural processes, these births can take place too early. These premature births may cause problem situations in the educational process. They may also disturb or even prevent a complete realization of the ego in later stages of life. Astral forces that are roused too early may be a serious threat to the ego. The ego, in such cases, will not be able to manifest itself to the full, which is in fact the aim of life. Dormant talents may be lost; the process of individuation, as Jung called it, may get blocked.

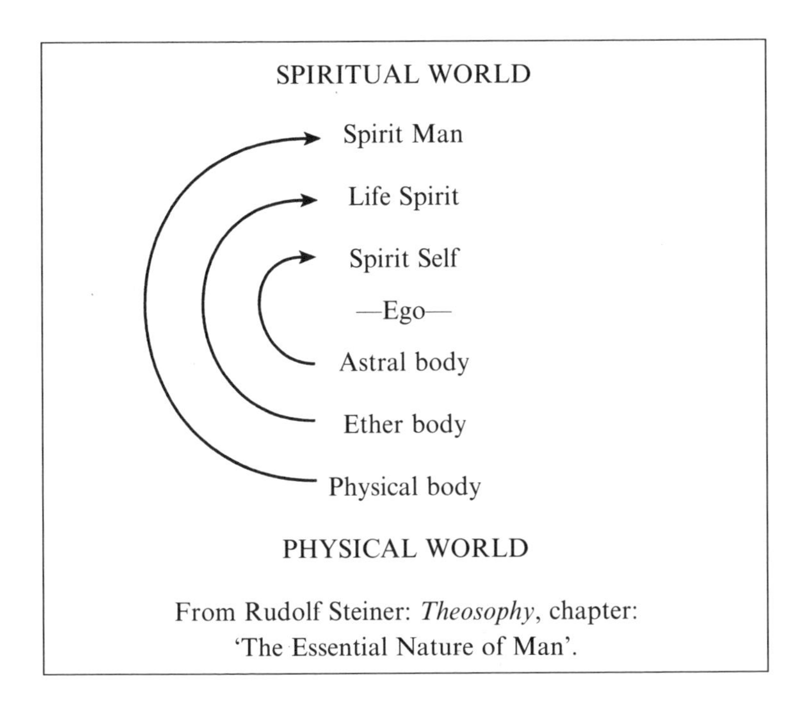

From Rudolf Steiner: *Theosophy*, chapter: 'The Essential Nature of Man'.

The central function of the ego is also expressed in one of Steiner's meditations:

Through the wide world there lives and moves
The real being of man,
While in the innermost core of man
The mirror-image of the world is living.

The ego unites the two,
And thus fulfils
The meaning of existence.

From Rudolf Steiner, *Verses and Meditations*

During the general course of life, the four members of the human being—the ego, the ether body, the astral body and the physical body—are liable to change. The ego, as it develops into one's personal biography, influences the other three members. The ego appropriates the altered parts of these members. Human beings learn how to handle the impulses that originate from the three other members. In doing so, these members are partially humanized. One can, for example, suppress the feeling of hunger for a while and wait until the other members of the family have arrived in order to have a meal together, instead of sitting immediately at the table alone. This is just one simple example of how the astral body can be mastered and be humanized by the ego. The part of the astral body that has been humanized in the course of life is called the *Spirit Self*.

A similar process goes on in the ether body. Habits, for instance, partially shape the ether body. We might say that every habit leaves an imprint in the ether body. If a human being breaks an ingrained habit he appropriates a part of the ether body. He makes it listen to the ultimate wish of the ego.

The part of the ether body that has been humanized in this way is called the *Life Spirit.*

In the physical body a similar process also takes place. When we take a good look at elderly people we can clearly see what the ego has done with the physical body over the years. This applies to the face in particular. The face is most strongly influenced by the ego. For this reason it is sometimes said that the human face is the thinnest possible membrane between the physical and the spiritual world. The part of the physical body that has been humanized in this way is called the *Spirit Man.*

These three processes develop extremely slowly and are difficult really to notice. Nevertheless they are real and they are essential parts of the anthroposophical image of man. These transformational processes may be considered the initial aim of life on earth.

The Four Temperaments

The four members are rarely divided equally in human beings. More often than not, one of the members prevails. To the trained eye this unequal division is clearly visible in young children. The prevailing member is likely to mark the total behaviour of the child. Educators could easily mistake this prevailing member for the supposed character of the child. Temperaments in children stand out clearly because the real ego is not yet manifest. As the child grows up, we may hope that the fully grown ego takes over more and more and that it harmonizes the influences that spring from the four members. Although humans never free themselves completely from these temperamental influences, the ego in the adult must overcome influences from the temperaments when they are too strong.

This phenomenon was also noticed by the Greek philosopher Empedocles (484–424 BC). He called this fourfold division: the four temperaments.

Prevailing member	**Temperament**	**Element**
Physical body	melancholic	earth
Ether body	phlegmatic	water
Astral body	sanguine	air
Ego	choleric	fire

The elements characterize the related temperaments in a rather sophisticated way. In his methodological lectures Rudolf Steiner points to this age-old wisdom and gives many indications as to how this knowledge can be used nowadays in educational situations.

It should be added that in the table above the word 'ego' refers to the so-called *lower self*. The ego is thought to consist of two parts: the *lower self*, this being the day-to-day experience of self-awareness, and a *higher self*, the more or less hidden part which one may become aware of when trying to analyse one's own or somebody else's biography. Much more is said by Dr Steiner regarding this twofold character of the ego, but this is beyond the scope of this book.

3. The Threefold Image of Man

When we look at a human being from yet a different angle, we can distinguish three parts: body, soul and spirit. The four members of the human being that have been discussed in the previous chapter can be related to this threefold division:

Physical and ether body	*body*
Astral body	*soul*
Ego	*spirit*

When we take a closer look at this threefold division, we get to know more about the origin of these entities. By standing on a high mountain, so to speak, we get a better view of the landscape. We are able to discover deeper layers of human nature.

One question: *Where do children come from?*
Two answers: *They are brought by the stork!*
They grow in cabbages!

Two old wives' tales which, each in its own way, tell the truth, as we shall see.

The physical body is born from the genetic material passed on by parents over many generations. The ether body, which maintains life in the physical body, can in this context be seen as part of this physical body.

Considering the story of the cabbage as an answer to the question above, the following can be said. When we look at the flower of a cabbage we see a cross of four petals. The number four also refers to the four main bearings of the compass that guide us across the earth. When we fill our nostrils with the smell of this flower we can easily imagine ourselves in a dank, musty cellar, well below the surface of the earth. We can safely say that this plant belongs to the earth rather than to the heavens. What a difference the image of the stork evokes! From the skies so high above it brings with it a heavenly message.

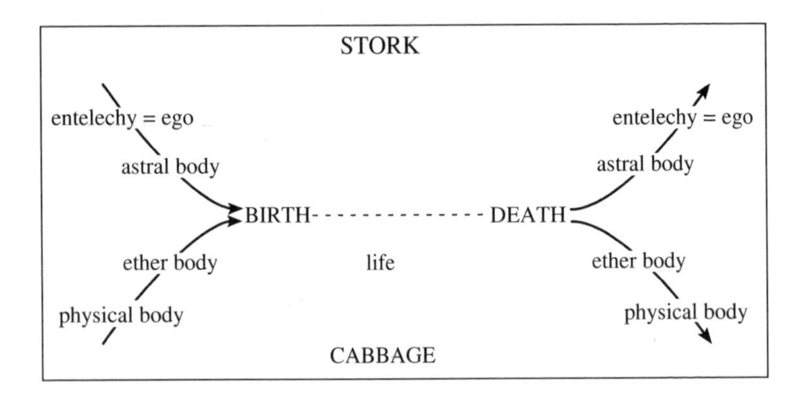

J.W. von Goethe compares the coming and going of the human soul—we had better say 'spirit' here—with the cyclical process of water.

> The human soul is like water,
> It comes from the heavens above,
> Whither it goes back after,
> And again to the earth it goes,
> In eternal change.

The story of the cabbage refers us to the origin of the physical body. The story of the stork tells us about the ego that is brought from the spiritual world to the physical world. At the moment of birth there are two components: the body and the ego. In anthroposophy the ego is considered to belong to the concept of *spirit*.

The moment a human being is born, he reacts to the whole range of sense impressions: air, light, cold, warmth, gravity, etc. This extensive complex of reactions to the physical world is called *soul* in anthroposophy. Thus, a human being consists of three components: *body, soul* and *spirit.*

Steiner points out that at the Council of Constantinople in AD 896 it was decided that human beings consist of two parts (also called dichotomy): *body* and *soul.* One of Steiner's missions was to explain that human beings consist of three parts: *body, soul* and *spirit* (also called trichotomy).

From anthroposophy we can learn that the ego originates from the spiritual world, where it resides between two lives. When the next incarnation is imminent it searches for a possibility to be born on earth. With the help of the angelic hierarchies the ego gives shape to the astral body, the ether body and the physical body. It should be clear that the final form of the body is conceived under the influence of the previous lives the ego has had before. On death the ego leaves the body again, returning to the spiritual world. The physical body is given back to the earth. The ether body dissolves in the ether body of the earth. The astral body eventually dissolves in the astral world. Only the ego, as a spiritual element, is not lost. It takes with it all the proceeds of the life that has just ended. It starts a new life in the spiritual world, where it dwells among spiritual beings preparing for yet another life on earth. Thus anthroposophy presents us with the age-old concept of *reincarnation.*

It is not easy to get a clear picture of this threefold image of man, consisting of *body, soul* and *spirit,* as the accepted western concept suggests a twofold image: *body* and *soul.* The following table may help us visualize this threefold character of a human being.

Physical	**Soul**	**Spirit**
An apple	*I like this apple*	*In every core we see a five-pointed star: a pentagram*
A snow crystal	*I admire its beauty*	*It is six-pointed: a hexagram*
A star	*I find it beautiful*	*Stars move according to fixed laws*
A rose	*I love the smell*	*There are always five sepals*

From these examples it may be clear what is meant by *body*, *soul* and *spirit*:

Physical:	the physical shape of the object itself
Soul:	my reaction when I perceive the object
Spirit:	the laws or regularities that are always present, independent of my reaction

Quite a puzzle!

The Golden Section or Sectio Divina can be found everywhere in nature. For example, in the spiral of the nautilus shell. The spiral develops according to fixed proportions.

Snow crystals, anywhere in the world, always have the shape of a six-pointed star.

Over the years many philosophers have discussed the hidden spiritual concepts that lie behind all physical forms. We can only understand the enigmatic form of an empty snail shell, which was shaped according to the ratio of the so-called Golden Section, when we envisage the animal that gave the shell its shape. In the same way, we can only understand all shapes and forms of the physical world when we relate them to the invisible formative forces that originate from the spiritual world. These invisible forces, for example, give any snowflake the shape of a six-pointed star.

Another attempt to understand these complicated processes is the following comparison. The waves in the sand on a beach can only be understood if we take into consideration how the sea, when the tide was in, gave shape to these sand waves. We even have to look to the wind that moved the water and to bear in mind that the sun caused the wind to blow. Consequently, the waves in the sand have ultimately been caused by the sun.

The German poet Friedrich Schiller (1759–1805) writes in his play *Wallenstein*:

> *'Es ist der Geist der sich den Körper baut.' ('It is the spirit that builds up the body.')*

The English poet John Dryden (1631–1700) takes this line of

thought a step further and writes that the ultimate force behind this formative process is, in fact, music:

'From harmony to harmony this universal frame began.'

This concept is not new. Pythagoras (sixth century BC) also mentions the musical origin of the universe. He shows that the mutual relationships between tonalities are in fact based on a numerical system. This idea suggested the concept of the *Harmony of the Spheres*.

J.W. von Goethe (1749–1832) considered all things transitory to be images of something spiritual.

'Alles Vergängliche ist nur ein Gleichnis.' ('All things transitory are resemblances of something else.')

Body, soul or spirit?

Which of these three concepts are expressed in the sentences below?

1. I do not like red tulips.
2. The three angles of a triangle together make 180 degrees.
3. There are ten roses in this bunch.
4. In the core of an apple we can discover a pentagram (a five-pointed star).
5. The length of a piece of string determines the pitch.
6. There are many Greek temples on the island of Sicily.
7. Every tulip has six petals.
8. I find tigers beautiful animals.
9. Five of these apples make one kilo.
10. I think that this room is too long and too narrow.

The answers:

Body: 3, 6, 9
Soul: 1, 8, 10
Spirit: 2, 4, 5, 7

Similarly, in the works of Plato (427–347 BC) we read about the concept that all things visible are resemblances of things spiritual. Plato attempts to explain this with his famous 'Myth of the Cave'. Let us imagine some human beings imprisoned in a cave. They are firmly chained on chairs and they can only look at the back wall. Behind these people a fire is burning. Between the fire and the prisoners all kinds of things are happening. The result of this arrangement is that the chained people see all sorts of moving shadows on the wall of the cave. Because they have never seen anything else, they take these shadows to be their reality. This is exactly our situation, according to Plato. We only perceive shadows of something spiritual. We cannot see this spiritual world because we do not have the required organs.

In 1787 the German physicist Ernst E.F. Chladni (1756–1827) published a book entitled *Entdeckungen über die Theorie des Klanges* (Discoveries about the theory of

Plato tried to explain to his students that all the things we see are mirror images, or shadows, of invisible spiritual entities.

sound). In this work he described how it is possible to make sound visible to the eyes. He strew fine sand on a metal plate. Next he gently brushed the edge of the plate with a bow so that the plate started to vibrate. To everyone's amazement the grains of sand jumped up and down and organized themselves into beautiful patterns depending on the pitch that was produced. This simple test has been repeated endlessly over the years in many physics lessons. Instead of sand, semolina can be used.

The German researcher Alexander Lauterwasser carries out similar experiments nowadays. He manages to show, and photograph, beautiful patterns in water which is brought into vibration by the sound from a loudspeaker. The pitch of the sound determines the shape of the pattern.

The creative invisible world of sound—of music, if you like—behind the physical world as it appears before our eyes is the main cause of the endless variety of all shapes and forms in nature.

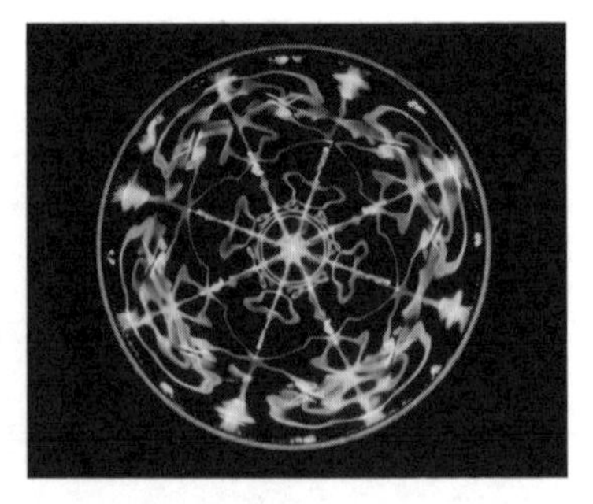

Ernst Chladni (1756–1827) carried out many tests to show that sounds can produce all sorts of shapes in loose sand on a flat plate (left). The results are called 'Chladni Figures'. Right: photo of a figure in a specially prepared liquid caused by sound. These sorts of tests are carried out by Alexander Lauterwasser and take Chladni's work a step further.

Rudolf Steiner, Pythagoras, Plato, Schiller, Dryden, Goethe, Chladni, Lauterwasser, and with them many others, try to explain to us the same phenomenon: behind all things created, a real spiritual world exists. Our ego, which travels from incarnation to incarnation, originates from the same world and is incessantly inspired by it during its life on earth.

The English poet William Wordsworth (1770–1850) also knew something of the spiritual origins of creation.

Our birth is but a sleep and a forgetting.
The soul that rises with us, our life's star,
has had elsewhere its setting
and comes from afar.
Not in entire forgetfulness,
not in utter nakedness,

but trailing clouds of glory
do we come from God who is our home.
Heaven lies about us in our infancy.

From *Intimations of Early Childhood*

4. Thinking, Feeling, Willing

Having discussed the fourfold and threefold concepts of man, we will now have a further look at the way in which a human being can act on earth among his fellow human beings. In anthroposophy we distinguish three areas in which human beings can act and express themselves: *thinking, feeling* and *willing*. Steiner links these three areas to the human body in the following way:

Head	*thinking*
Trunk (from neck to diaphragm)	*feeling*
Limbs and digestive system	*willing*

Characterization

A characterization of the *head* could be as follows:

Awake—In the head a human being is fully awake. It is here where clear thinking is localized.

Stationary—The head does not really move. If it did it could not enable human beings to think properly.

Cool—There is an old saying: 'Keep your head cool and your feet warm'. To be able to think properly the brain must not get hot. A hothead easily loses self-control.

The senses—In the head the senses are amply represented: eyesight, hearing, taste, smell.

Outside hard, inside soft—The soft brain is effectively protected by the hard bones of the skull. In the head a human

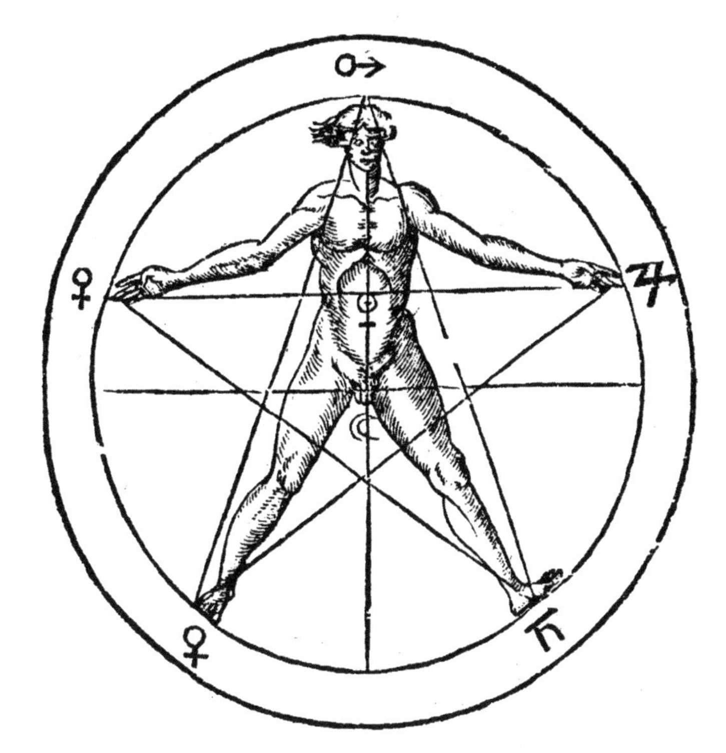

From 'Book of Occult Philosophy' by Agrippa von Nettesheim (Heinrich Cornelius), 1486–1535.

being is a sort of hermit. In old stories a castle often serves as a metaphor for the kind of person who is locked up within his own soul.

A characterization of the *limbs* and the *digestive system* could be like this:

Sleep—We are not aware of the digestive processes in our own body. When we do become aware of these processes we will be suffering pain somewhere in the body: headache, stomachache, etc. In other words, we have consciousness in the wrong place. Somebody with a stomach ulcer tries to understand the world with his stomach, which is not a good thing because the stomach is not a sensory organ. There should not be any awareness at all. And, of course, we know where our feet are but we do not think of our feet at every step. Too much awareness of the act of walking would hamper our movements.

Movement—The limbs suggest movement in all sorts of ways: gestures to amplify a line of thought, walking, writing, etc. And in the digestive organs movement is essential. Bowel movement is crucial to good health. The English word 'stool', for excrement, is quite appropriate. It is derived from 'going to stool', i.e. going to the toilet seat.

Warm—Belly and feet must be kept warm. Metabolic processes can only be successful in warm surroundings.

Blood—Blood is the dominating factor here. The nervous system is in the background.

Outside soft, inside hard—The legs are soft on the outside, the hard bones are inside. With the help of the limbs a human being can act as a social creature. With the limbs he makes his way amidst other human beings.

A characterization of the *trunk*—the area between the head and the digestive system—is that the two areas described above meet in a rhythmical sequence.

Breathing and the beat of the heart are linked in a rhythmical way. The systole (contraction) and the diastole (expansion) alternate in the heart. Neither the head nor the digestive system get the chance to continue their own tendencies without interruption. We can more or less regulate our breathing. When we concentrate and practise regularly we can influence our breathing quite strongly, but never to the same degree as we master the movements of our arms and legs.

In this rhythmical area we have a dreamlike consciousness. We are only half-aware of all the processes that take place there. Another characteristic of this area is that it is almost indefatigable: the heart beats, all life long.

Some more characteristics

In *Study of Man*, a course Steiner gave to the teachers of the first Waldorf School in Stuttgart in 1919, unexpected connections are demonstrated in relation to this threefold image of man. Steiner explains that the forces that are active in the head are of a contracting nature. The forces that are active in the limbs and digestive system have an expanding tendency. If in a child the upper forces are the stronger, the head may be relatively small. If on the contrary the lower forces are stronger, the head may be relatively large. This is not meant as a typology but merely to draw attention to a tendency, which implies that many variations are possible.

A child with a relatively small head has a tendency to like to know everything. Such children often like order and regularity. They like to have a pencil with a sharp point with which they can make clear and clever drawings. Frequently these children are real observers, they do not miss anything. They do not have much colour in their cheeks and in winter they need extra warmth in one way or another.

A child with a relatively large head is often less precise, sometimes even chaotic. These children just get on with life and enjoy it. They may feel bothered by too many clothes because they are never cold. They can play, paint, sing and do handicrafts, with unhampered passion.

By giving this somewhat generalized description, the two—or rather three—polarities in a human being become clearer. This should not have a stigmatizing effect in any way whatsoever. The tendencies are simply there, sometimes very obvious, sometimes hardly visible. Steiner gave this information as a help for teachers and parents to understand a little more about their children.

The Greek god Apollo is associated with formative forces and stillness, qualities that characterize the head.

The Greek god Dionysus is associated with chaos and movement, qualities that characterize the digestive system and the limbs.

Apollo—Dionysus

Rudolf Steiner, and Friedrich Nietzsche before him, links the two polarities, the upper and the lower, to the Greek gods Apollo and Dionysus. The thinking polarity is linked to Apollo, the willing polarity to Dionysus. If we want to speak about the rhythmical alternation between these two polarities we could also define them as the *Apollonian* and the *Dionysian* forces that alternate.

The two polarities discussed above are expressed in the following two lists.

Apollo	**Dionysus**
David	Goliath
dwarf	giant
Asterix	Obelix
hypothermia	fever
thin	thick
Sancho Panza	Don Quixote
Stan Laurel	Oliver Hardy
devil	dragon
structure	chaos
skeleton	blood
death	regeneration
schemes	enthusiasm
pale	blushing

The list can go on infinitely as soon as the two qualities are understood. A striking feature is that successful pairs, for example actors, comic-strip heroes, literary characters, etc., often represent these two polarities. The audience apparently recognizes, either consciously or unconsciously, the synergy between the two.

Many educators will have noticed that their work in everyday life is more successful when they pay attention to these polarities. After having listened to the teacher in a quiet Apollonian way for a certain period of time, children will have an inner urge to move in a Dionysian way. After a refreshing Dionysian interval, they will have new energy to tackle a subsequent intellectual problem with their heads or to listen with renewed concentration. Education, or even management, based on this natural rhythm will have the best chance of success. Variation in food keeps us healthy. This also holds good for spiritual food: we should alternately 'eat' from the *Tree of Knowledge* and the *Tree of Life*. If we eat too much from one tree and forget the existence of the other, we will become unbalanced human beings. In other words, these two trees are present in our own bodies. They need to be properly cared for.

> *'And out of the ground made the Lord God to grow every tree that is pleasant to the sight and good for the food: the Tree of Life also in the midst of the garden and the Tree of Knowledge of good and evil.'* (Genesis 2:9)

The tadpole

Initially the young child draws the human figure as a so-called tadpole. The trunk is not there, we just see the head to which

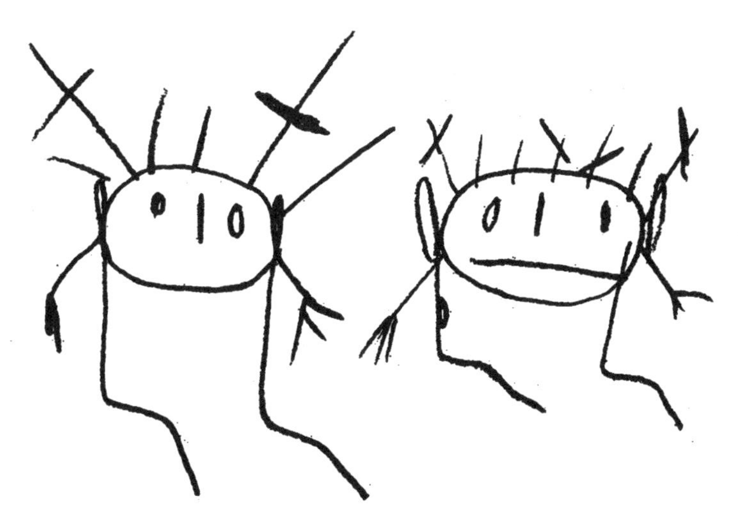

In this drawing of the so-called tadpole the trunk is missing. In small children the head is still connected to the digestive system. For this reason the head is not yet fully awake. The rhythmical part of the human body has still to conquer its own position between the upper and lower polarities.

the limbs are attached. In the sixth lecture of his *Study of Man*, Rudolf Steiner says about this phenomenon that such a creature can only move in a sort of sleep because the head is too attached and likewise influenced by the subconscious digestive forces. And this is exactly the developmental stage in which a child experiences daily life. Growing older is a waking-up process. Throughout the formative years human consciousness gradually but steadily loosens itself from these sleeping digestive forces in order to grow and become independent.

The rhythmical processes in the trunk must be further developed with the help of educators.

In *Study of Man* Steiner talks about the metamorphosis of the will: 'the thought is the metamorphosis of the will'. In the consecutive developmental stages in a child we can notice this metamorphic process. The development of thinking is preceded by the development of being able to stand and walk. As long as a child has to think about keeping the body upright, maintaining posture, placing the feet properly so as not to fall, the child will not be able to really think. The developmental stages are therefore: *walking—speaking—thinking*. If the forces of movement cannot be held back, if they are not firmly controlled, the development of thinking will not take place in the right way.

'By wagging its tail the dog loses its power of thought' is a well-known saying by Rudolf Steiner. Animals cannot restrain such drives. They cannot metamorphose this innate drive to move into powers of thought.

Initially the will and the faculty of thinking are still tightly linked in little children, as we have seen. In fact, the small child is controlled by the impulses that originate from the will and that cause strong feelings, such as hunger, thirst, pain, pleasure, etc. The process of becoming aware of the body is performed from top to bottom; it starts in the head. First the child learns how to focus the eyes, followed by awareness of the hands, then at last there is awareness of the feet. This process lasts approximately from 0 to 7 years. The period of 7 to 14 years is characterized by the development of feeling, which wedges its way between thinking and willing. Thanks to this newly acquired separation between thinking and willing, real conscious thinking can be developed. It is no longer influenced by the dormant powers of the will. The period of 14 to 21 years is characterized by the further development into mature thinking.

During all educational processes, as well as during life as an adult, these three areas, *thinking, feeling, willing*, have to be well looked after. Unfortunately nowadays, the human thinking qualities are over-stressed, resulting many a time in constrained, contorted situations. After all, if the powers of thinking, represented by the Tree of Knowledge, are called upon too much, the Tree of Life is bound to wither away because it does not get the chance to manifest its power. It is reined in, hampered, by the prevailing power of thought.

It is true that during sleep the consumed powers of life, also called the ether powers, are being replenished, but if overuse has taken place then this replenishment will not be sufficient. In a certain respect the thinking powers are dead, or deadening, forces. If these forces are given free rein, they will have a paralysing or fossilizing effect upon the body as well as upon the mind. In short, an unhealthy situation will result.

> *Think before you do*
> *And while doing keep thinking.*
> (ancient proverb)

Rudolf Steiner also characterizes these powers of thought as *antipathy powers*, and the powers of will as *sympathy powers.*

He tries to explain that a human being, in so far as he employs his will powers, in fact merges with the world. Suppressing this process, developing feelings of antipathy, will result in real human consciousness. Only when these powers of sympathy and antipathy are firmly balanced—kept in check by the ego—is real human life made possible.

In many forms of art we see this tripartite division:

EPIC POETRY	*APOLLO*	*THINKING*
LYRIC POETRY		*FEELING*
DRAMA	*DIONYSUS*	*WILLING*

Also in the symphony orchestra we see the same division:

WIND	*APOLLO*	*THINKING (HEAD)*
STRINGS		*FEELING*
DRUMS	*DIONYSUS*	*WILLING*

The conductor, facing the orchestra, represents the human ego leading all interaction between the three fields of power.

5. Man and Animal

In his book published in English as *Cosmic Memory*, Rudolf Steiner describes the consecutive stages of development of our solar system. When we read this description we should realize that the author did not draw on the usual sources, such as manuscripts or archaeological or astronomical discoveries that are available to everyone. Steiner was able to draw on a spiritual source which is called the Akasha Chronicle. Only people gifted with clairvoyant abilities are able to read in this ethereal book in which all events are recorded. To non-clairvoyant people the information that follows is unverifiable and therefore, according to present-day academic standards, unscientific. Be this as it may, the facts Steiner gives to the reader can be used as a working hypothesis. While studying all of this with an open mind the reader can decide which facts sound acceptable and which do not. It is often said that doubt is at the root of all science. To start with, we can give the benefit of the doubt to someone's theses and then see how far we can get.

The Akasha Chronicle is said to be a spiritual book in which all events that take place on earth are recorded. Some clairvoyant people are able to read in this ethereal book.

The following sequence of the developmental stages of our solar system is shown in Steiner's work:

Old Saturn
Old Sun
Old Moon

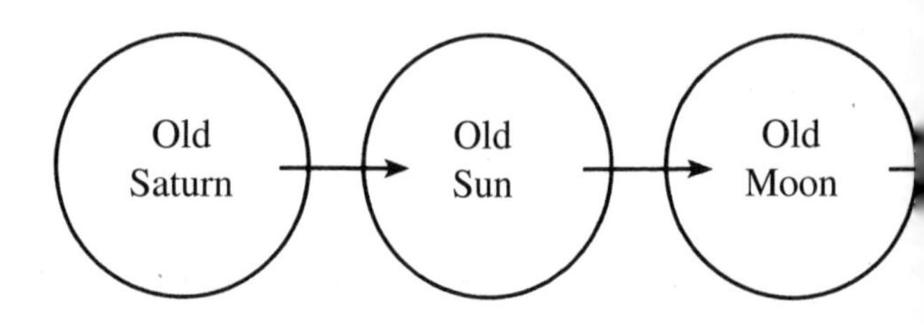

Earth (including Polarian and Hyperborean eras, Lemuria, Atlantis, Ancient India, Ancient Persia, Egypt and Babylonia, Greece and Rome, the fifth post-Atlantean period (= the present). Two future civilizations are to follow.
Jupiter
Venus
Vulcan

In *Knowledge of the Higher Worlds*, amongst other writings, Steiner describes the origin of our solar system. The nine so-called angel hierarchies are given the task by the Holy Trinity of undertaking the creation of the solar system. Invisible to our present-day eyes, these hierarchies start developing a complicated system that will eventually lead to the solar system as we now know it. The concept of 'time' is created simultaneously. This first system, which we might call the foundation stone, is called *Old Saturn,* named after the god of time; in Greek this god is called Chronos. At an embryonic stage, the process of creation is started with a spherical shape, having the density of 'warmth' (this being not a quality of something else but an extremely rarefied substance in its own right) and the size of the present orbit of Saturn. The spiritual basis of the human physical body is created. It is hardly possible, if at all, to indicate how long ago this event took place.

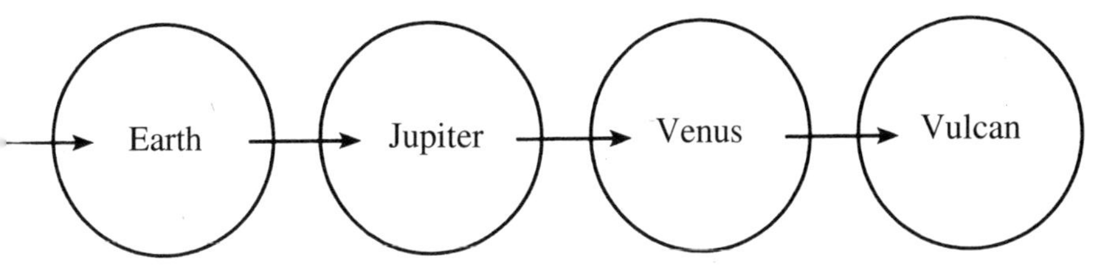

The seven developmental stages of our solar system, from Old Saturn, in the far-off past, to Vulcan, in the distant future.

This Old Saturn develops into a second phase, which Steiner calls *Old Sun*. The spiritual basis for the ether body is added. The angel hierarchies then further develop the physical body as well as the human ether body.

In the third stage, called *Old Moon,* the spiritual basis of the astral body is added. The hierarchies then continue their work on these three newly created members of mankind.

The fourth stage is called *Earth*. The preceding development is continued but now a fourth element is added: the human *ego*.

From the above it follows that we may call the human physical body the oldest member and the ego the youngest.

The stage called Earth, which is not yet our earth—the earth as we know it—develops further. Initially it is a coagulation of all the present planets, including the present sun. From this mass the present planets free themselves, one after another, until our earth is free and starts its own development. The various stages of this Earth stage are indicated by: Polarian era, Hyperborean era, Lemuria and Atlantis.

As soon as the word *Atlantis* is mentioned in this complex sequence, we can give an indication as to dates. Steiner tells us that human life on Atlantis existed from 50,000 years BC until approximately 10,000 years BC, when it was engulfed by an enormous tsunami and disappeared into the present Atlantic

Ocean. Many people managed to flee from the disaster, led by Manu and his seven Holy Rishis. They migrated along the present Mediterranean to the east and reached as far as India. The old stories of Noah and his Ark and of Utnapishtim, in the *Gilgamesh* epic, all point to this same event.

Rudolf Steiner highlights a number of civilizations that are created after the Atlantean disaster. These civilizations have been crucial in the overall development of human consciousness throughout the ages. The civilizations that Steiner mentions are the following:

Ancient India	*7227–5067 BC*
Ancient Persia	*5067–2907 BC*
Egypt–Babylon	*2907–747 BC*
Greece–Rome	*747 BC–1413 AD*
The fifth post-Atlantean period	*1413–3573 AD*

Two future civilizations are to follow. However, the development of our solar system will continue beyond this complete sequence of seven civilizations. The entire build-up of the system through the various planets will change. The present solar system is said to be developing into the new *Jupiter*. After this stage two more stages are to follow: the new *Venus* and finally *Vulcan*.

The development from Old Saturn to Vulcan, as we have described it, evokes a concept that can hardly be understood to the full. However, it is necessary to mention this concept because it is an essential part of anthroposophy. It is likely to crop up in all discussions on the anthroposophical view of mankind.

If we want to know more about the origins of the earth and mankind, we can seek out all sorts of documents which can serve as guides during this complicated search, guides such as these:

Palaeontology (fossils)
Comparative anatomy
Cultural inheritances (buildings, for example)
Rock-drawings (Lascaux in France, for example)
Mythologies
Embryology

And in the context of this book, we may add the Akasha Chronicle, the supersensible book in which Steiner, as an initiate, could read.

The name of Charles Darwin (1809–82) should certainly be mentioned here. His book *On the Origin of Species by Means of Natural Selection* was published in 1859. On the first day 1250 copies were sold. And still today the book is the subject of many heated discussions. According to Darwin, all forms of life on earth have come about as a result of natural selection, resulting from the struggle for life in which the fittest is the most likely to survive. Human beings came about in the same way, according to Darwin. Or to put it more specifically, man evolved from the higher primates. So, no divine *creation,* but *evolution.*

This area of discussion, which arises whenever man and animal are compared, is also expressed in the following quotation from *Pensées* (Thoughts) by the French mathematician and philosopher Blaise Pascal (1632–62):

> *'It is dangerous to show man how like he is to an animal if one does not show him his grandeur at the same time. Similarly, it is dangerous to show him his grandeur and not at the same time his turpitude.'*

The French palaeontologist, priest and philosopher Pierre Teilhard de Chardin (1881–1955) suggests, in *Le Phénomène Humain* (The human phenomenon) published in 1958, that the planet earth was created at a point which he calls *Alpha* and that the whole solar development moves from this diverging start to a converging point, which he calls *Omega*. Although there are Darwinian elements in his works, Teilhard de Chardin adds a spiritual element. He supposes that behind all creative processes we may find spiritually directing forces or even one single determining spiritual force. We can find parallels between his works and Steiner's way of thought.

Rudolf Steiner places the development of mankind in the overall development of the universe from Old Saturn to the future Vulcan. Mankind is the supporting axis throughout this amazing sequence. From the very beginning to the very last moment, man is involved. A clear understanding of Steiner's concept of *spirit* cannot be ignored if we are to understand this phenomenon. (See also chapter 3.)

According to Steiner everything related to knowledge of the physical world, in the widest possible sense of the word, comprises everything that was 'cast out' from the spiritual world straight into this physical world, as we know it through our usual senses. By way of comparison, a visible ice cube may be looked upon as invisible vapour in a different form. All things measurable and weighable are *states of aggregation* of something else. If we only study these final states of aggregation, i.e. the physical world (the world that can be perceived with our usual senses), we will never reach the origin. We can, for instance, knock down a building and study every single brick but in doing so we will never discover the creative, formative thoughts of the architect. Under a microscope, we can see what is 'not spirit'. A poet called this sort of science 'winter science', which leads us to yet another comparison. In winter, flowers of frost may be seen on a window pane. These flowers consist of mere water, it is true, but the question is: where do the shapes

Frost flowers on a window pane. They consist of mere water. The question is: where do the shapes come from?

come from? And why these shapes, the shapes we see at this particular moment? The source of the shapes is invisible to the untrained eye.

In order to understand something of the development of man, we must enter into this world which is not readily visible. Steiner tells us that on Old Saturn the development of man was initiated by the Holy Trinity and carried out by the nine angel hierarchies. However, in order to properly undergo this development, impeding elements had to be excluded from this process. These elements were disassociated, separated from the mainstream. This process of disassociation is essential for a good understanding of the anthroposophical way of thought. It continually took place throughout the planetary stages described in anthroposophy. This is difficult to grasp because the separating process occurred in the invisible spiritual world before the visible forms had materialized on earth.

Man was involved from the start and he is the essential, supporting axis of the whole process.

Man is not a final product, but was involved from the start in the creative processes of the hierarchies. Dr Hermann Poppelbaum elaborates on this anthroposophical concept in his book *Man and Animal.*

The following image may further help us understand this complicated concept. Let us imagine that the human nucleus is located in a huge downward-gliding balloon. This human nucleus must be developed further in a certain direction before this balloon lands on the newly created earth. The balloon is gradually gliding towards the earth. However, the landing on earth is continually postponed because certain elements are separated from this human nucleus and thrown overboard. In this way the landing is postponed and, at the same time, more space is made for further development of the nucleus. This process goes on and on. In succession, the minerals, the plants, the invertebrates, the fish, the amphibians, the reptiles, the birds, the lower mammals, the quadruped mammals, the primates and, finally, man are thrown out of the balloon. The whole development takes place simultaneously on two levels: on the spiritual level the forming human nucleus gradually glides towards the earth in this imaginary balloon, and on the physical level we see the materialized forms appear on earth.

These forms, materialized in earthly circumstances, develop further according to terrestrial laws. As soon as the plants and the animals appear on earth they are liable to further development in accordance with the laws that Darwin has discovered and called 'evolution'. The animals of the present are the result of age-old specialization. Every animal is a specialist. Some examples:

An animal is imitated by man in his tools.

Parrot	*bill*	*pair of pincers*
Woodpecker	*bill*	*hammer*
Eagle	*talons*	*grab crane*
Mole	*paws*	*scoop*
Horse	*leg*	*wellie*
Bird	*wing*	*plane*
Kangaroo	*tail*	*pillar*
Tiger	*eyetooth*	*dagger*
Cat	*molar teeth*	*scissors*

Considered in this way animals have been stalled, snarled up in their own physical shape. An animal's speciality has

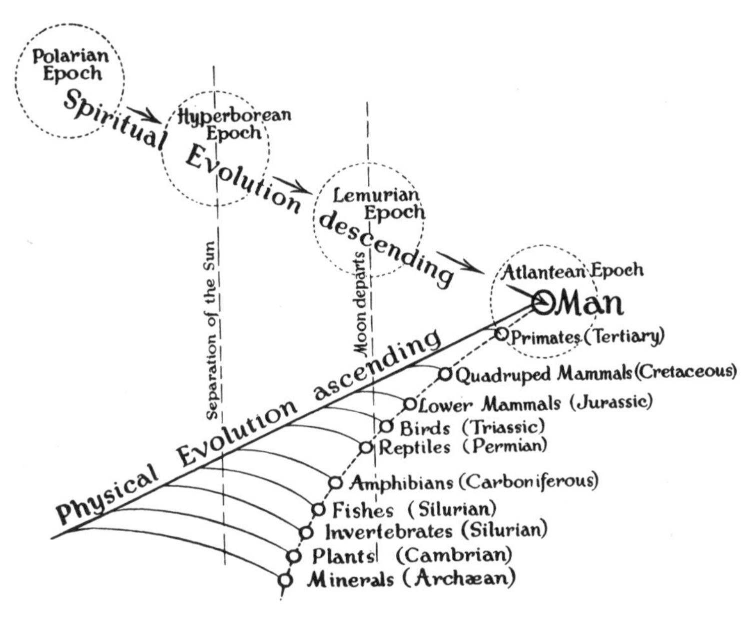

Illustration from Man and Animal *by Dr Hermann Poppelbaum. Man is the supporting axis in the development and was involved from the beginning.*

determined its outer physical form in such a way that it cannot do anything other than what its body allows. *Animals have lost their freedom.* Man, still present in this imaginative balloon, continues to postpone the moment of getting out and delays becoming part of the hardening process that will inevitably take place after landing.

In the table on page 55 we can see that the primates are the second-to-last to step out of the balloon and incarnate on earth. When the predecessors of man get out the imaginary balloon has almost landed. Among these predecessors we may mention Peking man (360,000 BC), Pithecanthropus (100,000 BC), and also Neanderthal man (75,000 BC). Remains of their skeletons have been found. Present mankind does not descend from these early beings and certainly not from the primates, as will have become clear from the previous explanation. When all these predecessors had landed on the earth and had materialized in earthly circumstances, only one spiritual element was left in this imaginary balloon. This last element lands on earth, so to speak, and gradually appears in the visible world as we now know it, approximately 50,000 years BC. This creature is usually called *Homo sapiens.* According to Rudolf Steiner the substance of these human beings, the last ones to get out of the balloon, was 'as thin as the scent of a flower'. In terrestrial circumstances the solidifying process went on and on. Gradually cartilage developed and, following this stage, real, more rigid human bones appeared.

If this development has really taken place, from an extremely thin, rarefied stage, through a stage of gradually hardening cartilage to, finally, extremely hard bones, it will never be possible to find fossilized remains of the early human beings because the material from which they were made was too soft, too easily dissolved—cartilage will not last long after death.

Human and animal forms

When comparing a human being to an animal the perpendicular gait of a human being is one of the most important differences we will notice. The human legs are fully occupied in resisting gravity. The feet are almost flat on the ground. The result is that the arms are totally freed from any supporting task. The arms are fully disconnected from gravity and enable a human being to act in a remarkably free way. This freedom is the most important characteristic of mankind. No animal can enjoy the total freedom of the front, or upper, limbs as human beings can.

Another testimony from which human development can be studied is *embryology*. When we study and compare the development of human and animal embryos we find it very striking to see that for a very short period the human embryo goes through stages that are remarkably similar to the stages of animal embryos. Very briefly, the human embryo is quite similar to that of a fish, quills and all, or of a bird, etc. The similarities are striking. Exactly by not adopting this passing animal shape the human embryo is able to develop further and further into the final human form. When the human being is eventually born, it turns out to be the most incomplete creature possible. It is the newborn, in all of nature, that is most in need of extensive assistance.

During his research, Teilhard de Chardin is confronted with the problem that he never succeeds in finding the precursors of the human beings of whom he finds the skeletons.

> *'Whichever group acts as the object of our observation, it always drowns in its own origin, in weakness, in the unsegmented. This is an infallible means to let disappear its stem in the genealogy.'*
> From: *The Phenomenon of Man.*

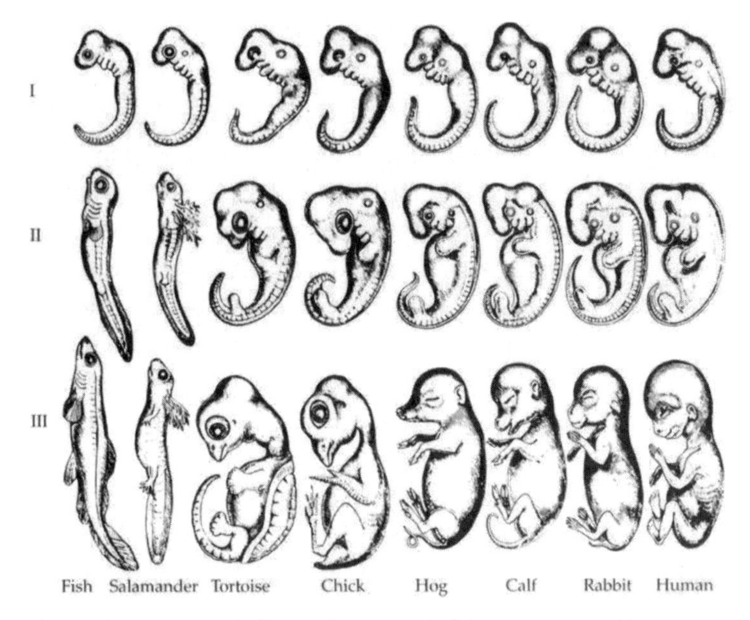

Chart of Ernst Haeckel *in relation to the development of human and animal embryos.*

When we summarize this chapter we could add that any human being, from conception to adulthood, repeats the development of mankind over the ages, from Old Saturn up until the present. This thought was also expressed by the German philosopher Ernst Haeckel (1834–1919). He is the author of the so-called biogenetic law or law of recapitulation:

'Ontogenesis is the repetition of phylogenesis'.

In simple words: *The development of an individual from germ cell to adulthood is equivalent to a shortened repetition of the stages which his predecessors have passed through from the very beginning of creation.*

Rudolf Steiner expands this biogenetic law by adding the previous planetary stages, as described above.

Pedagogical consequences

Rudolf Steiner's pedagogy is more or less based on this biogenetic law. Teachers choose the content of their lessons according to the psychological stage of development of their pupils. The world of the fairy tales, for example, surrounds the pupils until the age of seven. The Old Testament is the backdrop in Class 3, at the age of eight. In Classes 5 and 6, ages 11 and 12, the Ancient Greek and Roman civilizations are discussed. The voyages of discovery are the inspirational source in Class 8; and so on. The growing boy or girl repeats, in this way, the most important developmental stages of mankind and absorbs the essential knowledge and wisdom.

The ancestral sequence of mankind is the internal bond that keeps together the whole of evolution.

6. A History of Civilization: Seven Periods

Rudolf Steiner describes how the so-called Atlantean civilization disappeared in an enormous tsunami. A civilization that was started and maintained by initiated priests about 50,000 years BC was completely engulfed by the immense flooding of what is now called the Atlantic Ocean. Nothing was left. A whole civilization disappeared, in which people had had, at the onset, a physical body with the density of the 'scent of a flower' according to Steiner, and subsequently had a physical body with the density of cartilage. Those people had a sort of dreamlike consciousness. By day they were less awake and by night they were less deeply asleep, compared to the situation nowadays. They were not able to see the stars. Not only was their eyesight different, but the surrounding atmosphere was too humid, more like mist or fog, for them to be able to see the skies. They had been able to tap energy from fish eggs and use it to propel vehicles. The North Atlantic Drift still marks the place where it was located. Not only Steiner, drawing on the Akasha Chronicle, gives us these unusual details: Plato also mentions this sunken continent in his dialogues *Critias* and *Timaeus*. The fragmented and sometimes unclear information in Plato's dialogues concerning Atlantis is put into a broader perspective by Steiner's additions in his *From the Akasha Chronicle* (1905).

The well-known story in the Old Testament about Noah and his Ark full of animals also points to this enormous flood. We read too in this version of the events that God gives the rainbow to the survivors as a promise not to allow such a flood ever again. Apparently, after the flood, the atmosphere had cleared up—at least, had changed—in such a way that the rainbow became visible for the first time in the history of mankind.

> *'I do set my bow in the cloud and it shall be for a token of a covenant between me and the earth. And it shall come to pass when I bring a cloud over the earth that the bow shall be seen in the cloud.'*
> Genesis 9:13

In German mythology we also find a reference to this sunken continent of Atlantis. The name of *Niflheim* mentioned in the Germanic *Edda* may point to the mistlike atmosphere of Atlantis. (*Nifl* = mist, *heim* = home). Another reference is found in the Babylonian *Gilgamesh* epic, dating back to the third millennium BC. In this epic the leader who leads his people to safety is called Utnapishtim. The epic itself has come down to us in an incomplete way, but archaeologists have recently found fragments on clay tablets which have added new elements to the story.

After the Atlantean disaster, the so-called post-Atlantean civilizations begin. The classification is made according to the Platonic World Year, which lasts 25,920 years. In this period the spring equinox completes its run along the 12 signs of the zodiac. The dates mentioned are derived from this classification. (See page 50.)

Those who could escape the Atlantean disaster fled to higher ground on all sides of the Atlantic. The ancestors of the original inhabitants of the American continents must be sought on Atlantis. Steiner also mentions Manu, who with his Holy Rishis travelled via present-day Europe to Asia, crossed the Himalayas and founded a civilization in present-day India which in anthroposophy is called the first post-Atlantean civilization and lasted from 7227 BC until 5067 BC. In anthroposophy it is thought that present-day mankind is descended from Atlantean ancestors. The age-old skeletons that have been found in various places on earth originate from extinct human species. Their bodies were sclerosed to such a degree that they were not able to produce progeny. (See also page 54.)

Ancient India

Manu and his Holy Rishis organized the new civilization according to the caste system: priests, nobility, civilians, craftsmen, and the outcastes or pariahs. Even today this system maintains its influence in India.

In a clairvoyant way the priests received from their gods spiritual information with which they could lead their people. The divine texts they received in this way have become known as the Vedas. These voluminous texts, about six times the Bible in size, were and are considered to be a true revelation from the divine world. Although the content of the Vedas is age-old, these Sanskrit texts were only written down about 1500 BC on vulnerable palm leaves. Consequently, the content is much older than the manuscripts themselves.

Rudolf Steiner indicates that in the Vedas all divine wisdom that had been given to humanity until that developmental stage has been written down. Clairvoyance, present in all human beings at the time, started gradually to diminish but it was still possible, through these holy texts, to get in touch with the unseen spiritual world. This decrease of clairvoyance was due to a change in the four members of the people; the ether body, the astral body and the young ego were pulled gradually into the physical body. They experienced more and more the influence of earthly gravity. The process continued throughout the periods that were to follow.

In anthroposophy this is seen as pivotal in the overall development of mankind.

Krishna teaches Arjuna. He tells him that his ego is immortal and travels from incarnation to incarnation: *Just as a human being takes off his worn clothes and puts on new ones, the ego enters its new body after it has left its previous, mortal, earthly frame.*
Bhagavadgita, *chapter 2, verse 22*

In anthroposophy we can read the following characteristics of the *Ancient Indian* civilization. People did not experience a personal, well-defined ego. Their consciousness was totally different from ours. They were more at home in the spiritual world than in the physical world, the latter being said to be *maya,* unreal. The spiritual world, of which they were aware day and night, was felt to be the real world, their real home. They lived on everything the earth produced spontaneously: fruit, edible plants, honey, and milk from their cattle. Agriculture did not yet exist; they were nomads. When there was a flash of lightning they saw the spiritual creatures who caused it more clearly than the flash itself. It was a task of the priests to teach the people how they could see the flash itself and not the spiritual forces around it. The priests had to lead their people to earthly reality as we know it now.

A second collection of spiritual manuscripts is the *Mahabharata.* This is an enormous epic of 200,000 lines. It speaks of rivalry amongst various tribes. A well-known part of this epic is the *Bhagavadgita.* Rudolf Steiner explains some of the spiritual background to this story in which Arjuna, assisted by Krishna, has to combat his cousin Karna. In fact, according to Steiner, this story is about the battle of the human ego against the blood ties, the influence of which every human being has to overcome while growing up in order to make room for his budding ego. If these blood ties become too strong, the ego cannot manifest itself to the full. Arjuna, an excellent marksman, assisted by Krishna, defeats the threatening influences of the inherited blood, represented by his cousin Karna, and thus secures the way to further development of the human ego.

Krishna is the high divine counterpart of the human ego. This revelation takes place at a time when the young human ego is threatened with collapse under the hereditary forces of the blood.

Ancient India is a substantial and essential link in the development of human consciousness. That is why Steiner highlights this civilization which, of course, was not the only civilization on earth at the time. From the spiritual world, gradually and heedfully, the human ego descends into terrestrial circumstances. This is the process that is described in the scriptures of Ancient India. The development in India continues but, at a certain stage, the imaginary torch is handed over to the *Ancient Persian* civilization, which in anthroposophical terminology is called the second post-Atlantean civilization.

Ancient Persia

The Ancient Persian period lasts from 5067 until 2907 BC and is located mainly in the area of the rivers Tigris and Euphrates, in present-day Iran and Iraq. The main source of inspiration was Zarathustra. On closer examination we discover that there have been two individualities named Zarathustra. It would take us too long to explore this problem further but Rudolf Steiner points to the Zarathustra who lived about 5000 years BC as the instigator of Ancient Persia.

Ahura Mazda, the Great Aura of the Sun, on an arch of Xerxes' palace in Persepolis.

This important initiate was inspired by Ahura Mazda, the Great Aura of the Sun. In pictures we see him as a winged god who lives in the sun.

In Ancient India the whole of creation was felt to be just one single unity. In Ancient Persia, for the first time, people became aware of two polarities: dark and light. The darkness was said to be the realm of Ahriman, in opposition to the realm of light belonging to Ahura Mazda. The earth was no longer felt to be *maya* but a reality that can be worked on and tilled. Zarathustra is the founder of a new religion connected to the sun and he teaches his people how to cultivate apples from wild rose bushes, how to cultivate wheat from wild grass, to tame wild animals, to cultivate bulbous plants, etc. Zarathustra knows how to connect heaven and earth. Some more plants that originate from this ancient culture are: lettuce, cabbage, onions, parsley, leek, asparagus, pears, apricots, cherries, peach. For the first time, human beings, with the help of priests, learn how to till the earth.

The holy tradition of the Ancient Persians has come to us through the *Avesta*. In the oldest part of these scriptures we can read the *Gathas*. These are songs—mantras—that tell of Zarathustra's teachings. These songs have been passed on by word of mouth by his followers and had at the time magic powers with which wild plants could be brought to human use. After years of oral tradition the *Avesta* was written down on 12,000 cow hides and kept in the palace of Xerxes (485–465 BC) in Persepolis. Unfortunately the palace was set on fire by one of the soldiers of Alexander the Great (356–323 BC), resulting in the greater part of the *Avesta* being destroyed. Fortunately, a Greek copy was kept in Athens. Apart from some small fragments that arrived in the fifteenth century, the main part of the *Avesta* reached Europe in the eighteenth century.

According to Rudolf Steiner, the astral body was further developed into the sentient body during the Ancient Persian period. The former dreamlike consciousness had to be

In Ancient Persia the apple was cultivated from the wild rose. We still see the common pentagram in the core of an apple and in the sepals of a rose.

transformed into a clearer daylike consciousness with the help of the changing astral body. Due to this change the physical earth could be observed in a more conscious way. Mankind had to be taught to take a certain interest in the earth. At the same time, however, people were also confronted with the deadening forces of this self-same earth, the forces that solidify the spiritual creating powers into matter. These spiritual creating powers enter into another state of aggregation and become visible. The deadening forces that cannot be dispensed with are considered as belonging to the realm of Ahriman, an old Persian god.

Rudolf Steiner often lectured on Ahriman, the entity who on the one hand plays an essential role in the development of the earth, but who on the other poses a serious threat to mankind. All hardening processes, ossification, callosity, etc. are considered to be the work of Ahriman. The human skeleton, for example, is also the work of Ahriman. We meet these forces in particular in the human head, whereas in the digestive system and in the limbs we meet a force that gives warmth to the body, digests food, etc. This field of power is considered to come from *Lucifer*. In anthroposophy these two fields of power are considered to be counterpoints, which are clearly visible in a human being. Only when these two fields are well balanced will human beings be able to fully manifest themselves. Neither the cold and hardening nor the warm and dissolving polarity should prevail. Human liberty is linked to this delicate balance.

Followers of Zarathustra and the Ahura Mazda religion start to take flight from their land when Islam begins to spread in the countries around the rivers Tigris and Euphrates. They flee to India where, to the present day, they are called Parsis. Their religion still exists and is called *Zoroastrianism.*

Rudolf Steiner at work on the wooden statue, 'The Representative of Man'. The central figure of Christ holds the adversaries of Lucifer and Ahriman at bay.

Richard Strauss calls one of his tone poems *Also sprach Zarathustra*, after Nietszche's poem.

In his pedagogical lectures Rudolf Steiner mentions the similarity between this new awareness of light and dark and the developmental stage of children of about seven years old, in which for the first time the corporal differences between left and right come to light. In the framework of the biogenetic law mentioned above, we can say that such a child briefly experiences the same phenomenon as the Ancient Persians did in their day. Knowledge of ancient civilizations may help us to understand the psychological make-up of children while, on the other hand, knowledge of children may help us to understand how people experienced life in these ancient civilizations.

At table before a meal:

Thank heaven, thank earth,
so that everyone accepts
this wealth of food
which fills us with joy.
Thanks to the hands that prepared this meal.
Take with gladness,
peace and calm,
and remember that
only this will sustain our lives
that was blessed by man and God.

From: Zoroastrian science of nutrition

Ancient Egypt and Babylon

The third post-Atlantean period lasts from 2907 until 747 BC. Rudolf Steiner tells us about two cultures that take place at the same time: a twin civilization. In the Nile basin as well as in the basin of the Tigris and Euphrates civilizations develop that form an important link in the whole sequence of ever-changing human consciousness. As both the ether body and the astral body are pulled more and more into the physical body, clairvoyance strongly decreases. However, the desire for the spiritual world remains. This desire is an important characteristic for both civilizations.

In anthroposophy, the *Kali Yuga*—which is the name for the 'Dark Era'—is often mentioned. The term derives from Hinduism. It refers to a period of 5000 years that started around 3000 BC and lasted until about AD 1900. Steiner, in fact, mentions the year 1899 as the end of the Kali Yuga.

In this period man had to focus on the earth more and more. Direct awareness of the spiritual world had to be blocked. Man had really to get in touch with the earth. From

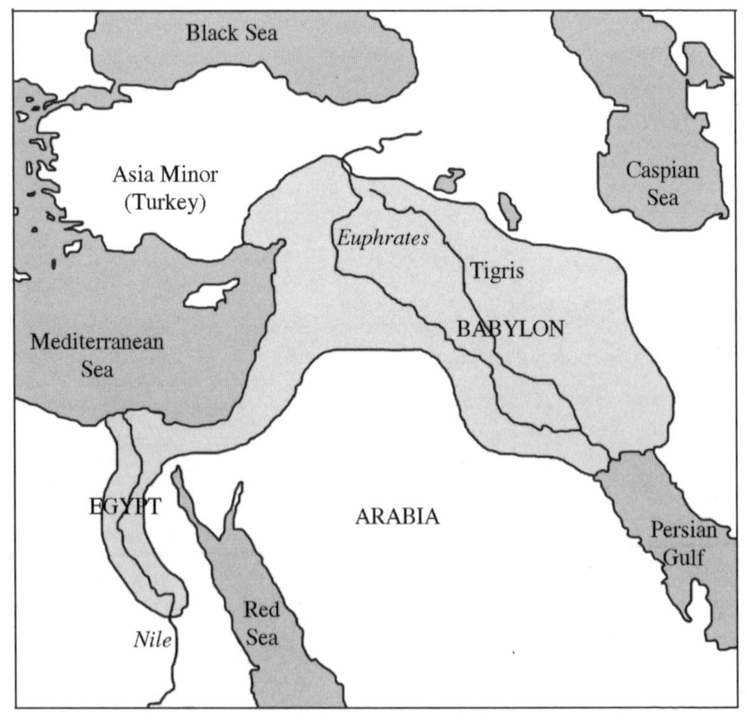

In the third millennium BC two cultures developed simultaneously: Ancient Egypt and Babylon.

Ancient Egypt onwards we see that, on the one hand, a technical development begins and, on the other, that people still try to stay in touch with the spiritual world that is disappearing more and more behind impenetrable veils. Only after 1899 the doors to heaven start slowly opening up again.

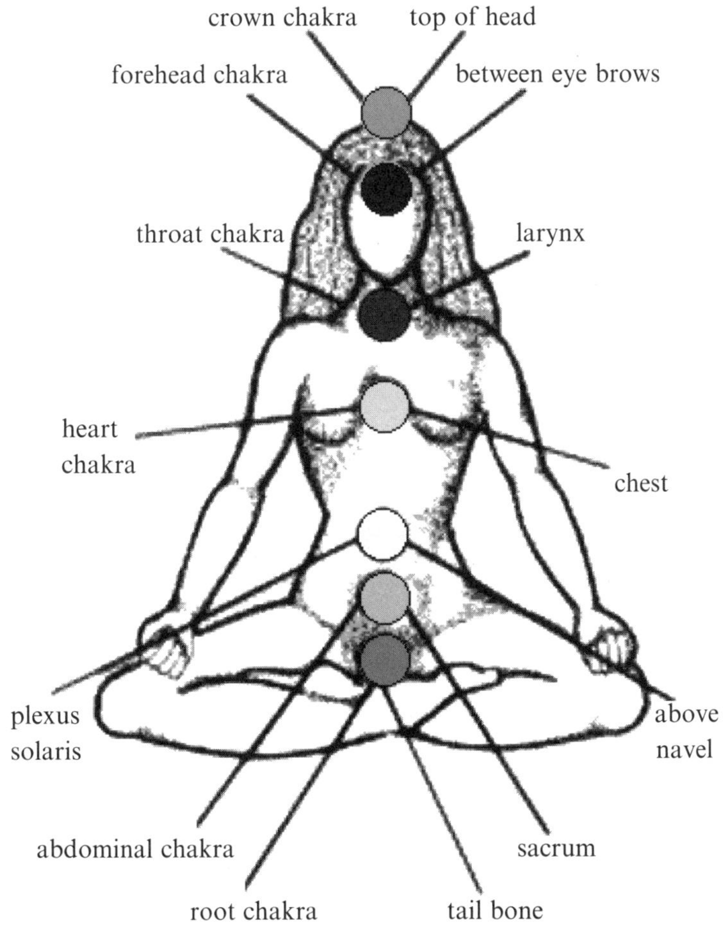

The seven main chakras. Clairvoyant observations can be made with these etheric organs.

From this moment on, the ether and astral bodies gradually start loosening themselves from the physical body, following which the ethereal organs, the *lotus flowers* or *chakras*, can resume their work, i.e. allow man to see into the spiritual world again. There is, however, a clear difference. The human ego is now involved in this act for the first time. Consciously the ego can and should be aware of this new way of observation. The human ego has grown and has learned a lot over the previous centuries.

Ancient Egypt

In 1799 the Rosetta Stone was found in the Nile delta. It is now one of the principal exhibits of the British Museum in London. On the stone we can read some texts in three different scripts: Egyptian hieroglyphics, demotic, Greek. The French Egyptologist Jean Champollion discovered that only one story was related in these three scripts. He managed to decipher the hieroglyphs in 1822 and opened up Ancient Egypt to modern scholars—nowadays we can read all ancient texts on all Egyptian monuments, papyri, etc. This quite recently acquired knowledge, combined with Rudolf Steiner's pointers, leads us to some crucial concepts which are described below.

Mummies

The remarkable and typically Egyptian mummy culture is related to the wish to remain in contact with the spiritual world. Due to this mummification process the soul of the deceased remained attached to the body for a longer period of time than was usually the case. With the help of the mummies the priests were able to get in touch with the spiritual world. The mummy became an artificial means to enter the world of the gods.

Thanks to the inscriptions on the Rosetta Stone, now in the British Museum, we are able to decipher the old Egyptian hieroglyphs.

Picture of the Egyptian Sun God Amon-Re with wings.

Initiation

During an initiation the neophyte was induced into a three-day temple sleep. When he awoke after this sleep, in which not only the ego and the astral body had left the physical body but the ether body had also partially abandoned the physical body, he was asked what he had witnessed in the spiritual world. The priests knew how to bring about such a state in the initiate with the help of all sorts of rituals. This loosening up of the four members of the initiate enabled him to observe otherwise invisible things. If an initiation failed, which sometimes happened, the priests felt utter disappointment. Initiation can be seen as an extremely difficult means to keep in touch with the divine world, which had been easily accessible in previous ancient civilizations, as described above.

Amon-Re

The sun was worshipped as the embodiment of Amon-Re, the sun god who moved across the sky in his barque from the east to the west. On many temples we see this god depicted as a sun disc with wings. The Ancient Persians, with their Ahura Mazda, as well as the Ancient Egyptians, were aware of the fact that the sun was not just a fiery ball in the sky. The sun was seen as the abode of a Divine Being. The Ancient Greeks also had their sun god, Helios, who travelled across the skies in his fiery chariot. We get the impression that all ancient civilizations must have had the feeling that there is far more to be said about this 'candle in the sky'. These peoples seem to have had a premonition of the fact that later on this sun god would come down to earth: Christ's birth in a human being. In Steiner's Christology, a relationship between the sun and Christ is dwelt upon extensively.

Isis, Osiris, Horus

The late Swiss psychiatrist C.G. Jung (1875–1961) tells us about the so-called *archetypes*. These are age-old images which appear in dreams and in mythologies. They point to spiritual realities with a profound meaning. One of these archetypes is the *Divine Child*. Through all ages and in all cultures we meet this archetype. At all times we see a masculine and a feminine element coming together and giving birth to a child. One of the possible explanations is the following.

In the overall process of creation, from Ancient Saturn to future Vulcan, the angel hierarchies are busy perfecting the human ego. This human ego, as the result of the spirit (as the masculine element) and the earth (as the feminine element), is this Divine Child. In Egyptian mythology the goddess Isis and her brother Osiris start a relationship and produce the divine child named Horus. This child represents the human *Higher Self*, which has yet to be developed from the present human ego. This Higher Self, the ultimate goal of life on earth, was briefly amongst us in Christ.

Joseph

In the Old Testament, in Genesis 41, we read about the Egyptian pharaoh who no longer understands his own dreams. All the magicians of the realm are summoned to court, but none can explain the dreams. Then Joseph, an imprisoned Hebrew boy, is taken before the pharaoh. He is able to reveal to the pharaoh the meaning of these dreams. In the preceding civilizations dreams belonged to the not yet locked away consciousness of the night. People remembered clearly where they had been during the night and could speak easily about these experiences. In Ancient Egypt, however, we see that only some gifted individuals could explain dreams: the Kali Yuga had begun.

Babylonia

The best known myth from Mesopotamia, present-day Iran and Iraq, is the story of Gilgamesh. The story is written on clay tablets which belonged to the library of Assurbanipal (668–626 BC), King of Assyria. Recently some more clay tablets once belonging to this library have been found. The *Gilgamesh* epic takes us to 3000 BC. Apart from the references to the Flood that swept Atlantis from the face of the earth, the story is also interesting in relation to Gilgamesh's unexpected confrontation with the phenomenon of death. When his best friend and comrade Enkidu dies, Gilgamesh anxiously queries: 'My brother, what sort of sleep keeps you as a captive?'

Babel became known for its hanging gardens and for its tower that was to reach Heaven. Pieter Brueghel the Elder (1525–69) made this painting in 1563.

Enkidu's soul, which had left his body, had apparently become invisible to Gilgamesh, something he had not expected.

Gilgamesh, although two thirds god and one third man, was no longer prone, just like the Egyptian pharaohs, to any clairvoyance. Death had become an enigma. The Tower of Babel is another example from which it may appear that the wish to get in touch with the divine world was extremely strong. Unfortunately this building project, initiated by Hammurabi (1810–1750 BC) was bound to fail. Man could not escape the earth and all its terrestrial influences.

Rudolf Steiner points out that in this third post-Atlantean period the so-called *sentient soul* is developed. Following the development of the *sentient body* (see also pages 66–7) man is now enabled to record with the help of this *sentient soul* all sense impressions in a newly established memory system which is located in the ether body. This process is well illustrated by the following brief historical overview. Initially, human beings need external anchors to be able to remember facts, figures, persons, etc. In the Bible, Genesis 28:18, we read that Jacob, after an impressive dream, erects a stone to commemorate his dream.

> *'And Joseph rose up early in the morning and took a stone that he had put for his pillows and set it up for a pillar (...)'*

In nursery schools objects are sometimes placed around the classroom to help memorize scenes from fairy tales. A dish with lintels, for example, when the story of Cinderella is being told. The next day a child can walk round the classroom among these objects and retell whatever fragments of the story spring to mind. Displays such as these are an important support that gives structure to the young child's memory in time and space.

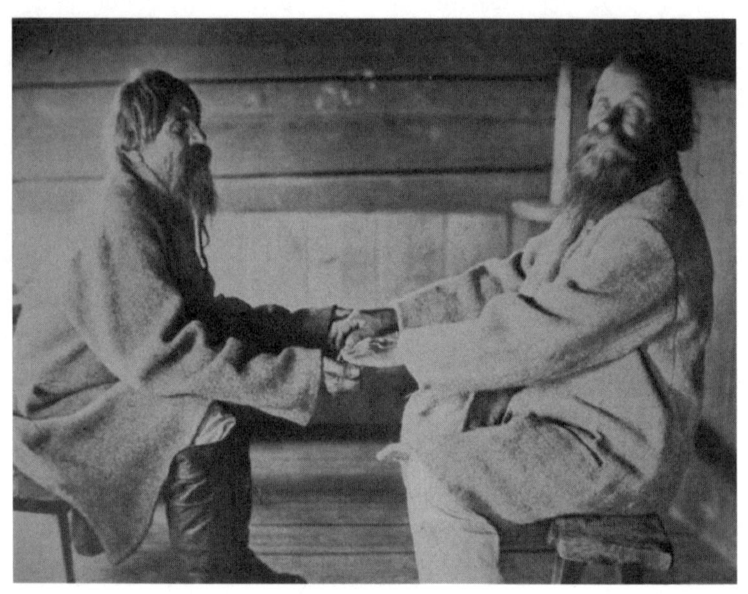

Nineteenth-century rune singers from Finland. They move in rhythm to the recited verses to support memory functions.

In fact all statues in our modern towns and villages have the same effect. When the functions of memory are internalized—when sense impressions are imprinted into the ether body, in anthroposophical terminology—we see that rhythm starts to support this process. Many old myths have long been recited aloud with a certain rhythm. In our present-day society memory has been fully internalized. Nowadays we can remember enormous numbers of facts without the help of external objects or rhythms.

Ancient Greece and Ancient Rome

The fourth post-Atlantean period lasts from 747 BC until AD 1413. The development of human consciousness will be further discussed now in the light of Ancient Greece and

Ancient Rome. The latter is followed by the Christian Middle Ages and an essential change in human consciousness takes place in the fourteen and fifteenth centuries: the Renaissance.

Ancient Greece

Rudolf Steiner gives 747 BC as the beginning of the new period. Others give 776 BC, when the first Olympic Games took place, as the starting date. With regard to these games Steiner tells us that the phenomenon of the 'winner' is created: the winner of a running event, for example. By winning such an event the winner is likely to gain extra awareness of his ego. And that was precisely what the gods had in mind. The very young human ego had to get an extra impulse to grow into earthly circumstances.

How clairvoyance decreased—had to decrease—is also illustrated by the story of the Cyclops Polyphemus. To escape from this monster-like giant with one eye, Odysseus decides to blind him. He takes a pole which he heats in a fire and thrusts it into the giant's only eye. This act represents the end of human clairvoyance, which was quite normal as we have seen. Odysseus represents the awakening human ego which becomes more and more focused on earthly matters and at the same time loses contact with the spiritual world. Clairvoyance had to disappear in order for present-day consciousness to develop. All human beings still have this third eye between the two physical eyes. It is the lotus flower, or chakra, with which clairvoyant observations can be made. Nowadays this chakra is inactive in most people, although in the future it will become active again, but with the ego as 'captain'. In order to develop independent thinking, independent of the gods, this clairvoyance had to disappear. Grimm's fairy tale of 'One-eye, Two-eye and Three-eye' has the same background.

The story of the labyrinth of King Minos on the isle of

Crete also points to the budding growth of man's independent thinking, independent of the gods. Ariadne's thread, thanks to which Theseus knows how to escape from the labyrinth, is an image, a metaphor of human thought that takes place in the convolutions of the brain—the labyrinth—as an independent process guided by the human ego.

In the Ancient Greek period, human beings start to think about thinking for the first time in history. Greek philosophy is born. Socrates, Plato and Aristotle can be called the founding fathers of this new step in the intellectual development of mankind. Plato compares man's situation on earth with the famous parable of the cave. On earth we see only shadows of the real spiritual world. (See page 33.) Socrates says: 'Become who you are.' For this remark he is sometimes called 'a spiritual midwife'. And with his ten categories Aristotle teaches 'the right way to human thinking'. Alexander the Great (356–323 BC) spreads the concepts of his teacher, Aristotle, across a considerable part of Asia, even as far as the River Ganges in India.

The threefold character of thinking, feeling and willing is found in many Greek sanctuaries. In Delphi, for example, we clearly see the temple complex (thinking), the theatre (feeling) and the stadium (willing). The archetypal basis of man is laid out in the landscape in this way. The Greek sanctuaries were also places where sick people could be cured by the well-balanced care of the three basic qualities of the human being. In anthroposophy, we see the same attention to this threefold character of man in Waldorf education and in anthroposophical health care.

Rome

The development of man's intellectual faculties that had started in Ancient Greece reached a provisional apex in

In this picture we can clearly see, bottom left, the temple (thinking), in the middle the amphitheatre (feeling) and on the right, somewhat higher up the hill, the stadium (willing).

Ancient Rome. At the peak of this civilization, human interest was entirely focused on earthly matters. From Roman remains it is evident that the Romans knew how to deal with all kinds of architectural problems. The Romans mastered many technical problems due to which their bridges, theatres, roads, aqueducts, etc. are still in place. When walking through Pompeii we are amazed by all the road constructions, water pipes, shops, houses, squares, etc. In our eyes the town even looks modern. It is amazing that such a town could have been built two thousand years ago. In spite of the many temples in the town, a true religious life seems to be absent. The Romans absorbed the religions of the people they conquered and they gave these gods new names. Original or seminal inspiration is scarcely to be found. The Kali Yuga stage of development is in full swing.

In this period, in which almost all contact with the spiritual world has disappeared, the so-called *intellectual soul* is developed. The ether body as well as the astral body had been absorbed into the physical body to such an extent that all the powers present in these two members could be mobilized to give man independent power of thought. Amidst this culture, in which hardening processes that focused on terrestrial matter increased, Christ was born.

Profit is Joy
Written on a wall in Pompeii, AD 100.

According to Rudolf Steiner the birth of Christ on earth was brought about by the Holy Trinity in order to bring this accelerating hardening process to a halt. If this had not happened the development of the human ego would have been endangered. Christ, the divine Logos according to the evangelist St John, gave the planet earth a divine Ego and by doing so Christ became the meaning and purpose of this planet. Only after three centuries was the new religion taken seriously. After a vision, the Emperor Constantine the Great (AD 272–337) declared Christianity to be the state religion throughout the entire Roman Empire. Eventually Constantine was baptized and became the first Christian Roman Emperor.

The Middle Ages, AD 500–1450

When the Roman Empire collapses, the carrier wave of the developing human consciousness moves to central and northern Europe. Again it is important to note that other civilizations are not negated by Steiner in his way of thought. It is a matter of highlighting: Steiner points to the leitmotiv that runs from one civilization to another and which indicates a long development from an initially blurred sort of consciousness to an independent consciousness lead by the ego.

Christianity leaves a mark on almost all cultural expression in Europe. On the one hand, Christianity points to the divine origin of humanity, and on the other, due to the abolition of the concept of 'spirit' at the Council of Constantinople in AD 896, Christianity strengthens the bond with earthly matters. (See also page 29.) When the established Church takes on too much power over the way people think, counter-movements arise. The Cathars, the Templars and the Gnostics may be mentioned in this context.

The fifth post-Atlantean period

In 1413 the fifth post-Atlantean period begins. Rudolf Steiner did not give it a special name. This period, according to the Platonic World Year, will last until AD 3573. (See also page 50.)

The change in human consciousness becomes clear in the Renaissance and in Humanism. People want to read and study old texts themselves, in their own language. As a result of the invention of the art of printing, in approximately 1450, the new ideas can spread rapidly around Europe. The discovery of America (1492) and Copernicus' discovery that the sun and not the earth is the centre of the solar system thoroughly change the way people look upon the creation of the world. In painting, the 'still life' appears for the first time. Man has developed such a distance between himself and the physical world that he can observe it as a separate object, entirely outside himself. He can observe all deadening forces—very often a skull is depicted in a still life—objectively. This had never happened before. Man had always been part and parcel of the world. Now the separation became manifest.

The Royal Society of London for the Improvement of Natural Knowledge was founded in Oxford in 1645 and was inspired by Francis Bacon (1561–1626). In spite of counter-movements such as the *Rosicrucians* at the start of the seventeenth century, the principles that all scientific research must be verifiable—everything must be weighable and measurable—culminated in the industrial revolution of the eighteenth century. After the attempt by the Rosicrucians, *c.* 1615, to counterbalance this rational approach to the world, a second attempt took place at the end of the eighteenth century. The French Revolution in 1789, with the motto Freedom, Equality, Fraternity, is considered by Rudolf Steiner to be a second attempt to bring back spirituality to everyday life. This attempt is not successful because Napoleon, according to Steiner, forgot his spiritual assignment.

At the end of the nineteenth century, a century full of exciting inventions, Kali Yuga is brought to an end in 1899. The human spirit, which had descended as deeply as possible into earthly matters, could again start the ascent towards more spiritual quarters. The four members of the human being loosen up again, are separated again, but this time the human ego is fully aware of the process. The human ego will become more and more able, albeit very gradually, to perceive the spiritual world which is the basis of all creation. After the development of the sentient body (Ancient Persia), the sentient soul (Egypt-Babylonia) and the intellectual soul (Greece-Rome), the *consciousness soul* starts developing in this fifth post-Atlantean period.

The influence of the human ego is discernible in the physical body, the ether body and the astral body. In fact, the ego reworks these three members. Parts are appropriated by the ego. Everything that has been reworked and thus appropriated will be taken through death by the ego on its way to the next incarnation. These reworked parts—Spirit Self, Life Spirit and Spirit Man (see also page 23)—determine what the ego, between two incarnations, can learn from the hierarchies among which he will be residing before he goes on his way again to earth. In this way the mutual relationships between the physical and the spiritual worlds become clear.

Man is not part of an endless, cyclical way of living but moves in a linear way with a clear aim. This aim is not readily visible, it is true, but Steiner's anthroposophy tries to be a *Golden Bough* with which man can carefully and heedfully open up the invisible, spiritual world which is the foundation of all things visible. Without wakening these slumbering faculties, man is destined to be fossilized and with this the earth, too, will be fossilized.

According to anthroposophy, the planet earth—called the Planet of Wisdom—will in a distant future metamorphose, as a consequence of all these processes, into the new Jupiter, the Planet of Love.

Epilogue

In the preceding chapters I have attempted to show the reader some important elements of Rudolf Steiner's anthroposophy, which attempts to shed some light on the cosmic wisdom that is hidden in any human being. The question is whether man is capable of discovering this inborn wisdom. Anthroposophy would like to be of some assistance during this breathtaking voyage of discovery. I have given the reader some basic concepts which can serve as tools during this exciting trip. But, as is always the case with new tools, one has to learn how to handle them. This may take some time. When it has become clear how to handle these new tools, it is a real pleasure to use them in everyday life. One's view of the world and all its inhabitants will change. New vistas open up. Then man will not turn out to be a traveller who has forgotten both starting point and aim of the journey through life. Anthroposophy sheds light on pre-existence, on life as it is now and on the world one will enter after life on earth.

Vast and impressive relationships are brought to light, through which unexpected depth is given to the meaning of life on earth.

Some Important Dates in Rudolf Steiner's Life

1861	Born in Kraljevec on 27 February
1872	Begins school in Wiener Neustadt
1879	Begins studies in Technical High School, Vienna
1891	Graduates from Rostock University with PhD
1900	Delivers first lectures
1902	Becomes Secretary of the German Section of the Theosophical Society
1913	Founds the Anthroposophical Society
1913	Lays foundation stone of first Goetheanum
1922	First Goetheanum burns down (night of 31 December)
1923/24	Christmas Meeting (*Weihnachtstagung*) takes place in Dornach
1925	Dies on 30 March

Further Reading

Fundamental works by Rudolf Steiner:
Knowledge of the Higher Worlds (also published as: *How to Know Higher Worlds*)
Occult Science (also published as: *An Outline of Esoteric Science*)
Theosophy
The Philosophy of Freedom (also published as: *Intuitive Thinking as a Spiritual Path*)

Other works:
Anthroposophical Leading Thoughts
Autobiography
Education of the Child
Study of Man

Other Authors:
J. W. Von Goethe, *The Green Snake and the Beautiful Lily, A Fairy Tale*
Hermann Poppelbaum: *Man and Animal, Their Essential Difference*

Available from Rudolf Steiner Press (UK) or SteinerBooks (USA).